WOMEN'S REPRODUCTIVE RIGHTS IN DEVELOPING COUNTRIES

TO

*My late father C. K. Unnikrishna Pillai,
my mother Chandramathi,
and my late sister Indira Menon.*

*My father Wang Zhi-liang,
my mother Zhou Yu-hua,
and sister Guang-lan who did not live to see this book*

Women's Reproductive Rights in Developing Countries

VIJAYAN K. PILLAI
University of North Texas

GUANG-ZHEN WANG
University of Arkansas at Little Rock

LONDON AND NEW YORK

First published 1999 by Ashgate Publishing

Reissued 2018 by Routledge
2 Park Square, Milton Park, Abingdon, Oxon OX14 4RN
52 Vanderbilt Avenue, New York, NY 10017

Routledge is an imprint of the Taylor & Francis Group, an informa business

Copyright © Vijayan K. Pillai and Guang-zhen Wang 1999

All rights reserved. No part of this book may be reprinted or reproduced or utilised in any form or by any electronic, mechanical, or other means, now known or hereafter invented, including photocopying and recording, or in any information storage or retrieval system, without permission in writing from the publishers.

Notice:
Product or corporate names may be trademarks or registered trademarks, and are used only for identification and explanation without intent to infringe.

Publisher's Note
The publisher has gone to great lengths to ensure the quality of this reprint but points out that some imperfections in the original copies may be apparent.

Disclaimer
The publisher has made every effort to trace copyright holders and welcomes correspondence from those they have been unable to contact.

A Library of Congress record exists under LC control number: 99072243

ISBN 13: 978-1-138-35918-5 (hbk)
ISBN 13: 978-1-138-35921-5 (pbk)
ISBN 13: 978-0-429-43382-5 (ebk)

Contents

List of Figures		*vii*
List of Tables		*ix*
Preface		*xi*
Acknowledgements		*xiii*
1	Introduction	1
2	State Population Control Policies and Reproductive Rights	11
3	Value Systems and Reproductive Rights	17
4	Women's Health Movements and Reproductive Rights	31
5	Overview of Rights in Classical and Contemporary Sociological Theories	37
6	Explanations of Reproductive Rights	43
7	Methodology	59
8	Analyses and Results	71
9	Post Hoc Modeling of Women's Reproductive Rights	101
10	Discussion and Conclusion	117
References		139
Appendices		151
Index		187

List of Figures

Figure 6.1	The proposed model of women's reproductive rights	55
Figure 8.1	Mean comparison of legal abortion right in 1992 and 1989	77
Figure 8.2	Mean comparison of marriage and divorce rights	78
Figure 8.3	Mean comparison of civil and intermarriage rights	79
Figure 8.4	Regional comparison of reproductive rights scores	80
Figure 8.5	Reduced model of women's reproductive rights	92
Figure 8.6	Women's reproductive rights: Q-plot of standardized residuals	96
Figure 9.1	The alternative model of women's reproductive rights: the effect of reproductive rights on population growth	102
Figure 9.2	Women's reproductive rights: a submodel of proximate factors	104
Figure 9.3	Women's reproductive rights: expansion of the submodel	105
Figure 9.4	Women's reproductive rights: reassessed version of the expanded submodel	107
Figure 9.5a	Path model of legal abortion right	112
Figure 9.5b	Path model of personal rights to interracial, interreligious, or civil marriages	112
Figure 9.5c	Path model of personal rights for equality of sexes during marriage and for divorce proceedings	113
Figure 9.5d	Path model of personal rights to use contraceptive pills and devices	113
Figure 9.5e	Path model of support for contraceptive use	114

List of Tables

Table 6.1	Variable names and definitions	56
Table 7.1	Data sources for the variables	60
Table 8.1	Frequencies, means, and standard deviations (N=101)	72
Table 8.2	Reproductive rights: a cluster analysis of developing nations (N=74)	81
Table 8.3	Unstandardized and standardized coefficients for OLS additive models of legal abortion right (standardized coefficients in parentheses)	83
Table 8.4	Unstandardized and standardized coefficients for OLS additive models of personal rights (standardized coefficients in parentheses)	84
Table 8.5	Correlations among indicators within constructs	86
Table 8.6	Intercorrelations among constructs in the reproductive rights model	89
Table 8.7	Measurement model parameters for women's reproductive rights (standardized solutions in parentheses)	90
Table 8.8	Structural model, LISREL estimates (maximum likelihood), unstandardized and standardized parameter estimates (standardized estimates in parentheses)	94
Table 8.9	Decomposition of causal effects	94
Table 8.10	Overall model fit indices	98
Table 8.11	Research hypotheses and empirical findings	99
Table 9.1	The alternative model, LISREL estimates (maximum likelihood), unstandardized and standardized parameter estimates (standardized estimates in parentheses)	103

Table 9.2	Submodels, LISREL estimates (maximum likelihood), unstandardized and standardized parameter estimates (standardized estimates in parentheses)	106
Table 9.3	Cumulative probit models for ABORTION, INTERRAC, DIVORCE, PILLS, and SUPPORT	109
Table 9.4	Cumulative probit models for ABORTION, INTERRAC, DIVORCE, PILLS, and SUPPORT controlling for regions	111

Preface

Reproductive rights and population control are among the most controversial and sensitive issues of the twentieth century. The focus on reproductive rights in the recent years, we argue, emerges from three distinct sources. They are the long standing human rights tradition rooted in Western values, worldwide population control programs, and the reproductive health movement. Human rights activists have brought to the attention of the world community gender specific risks such as domestic violence against women. Mounting accusations of coercive birth control practices brought about a political backlash and a renewed interest in voluntary fertility as a broad-based ethical foundation for population control programs. International reproductive health movements in the late 1970s and early 1980s criticized family planning programs especially in developing countries for focusing on achieving quantitative goals and neglecting women's reproductive health. Finally, it is now well recognized by medical and public health professionals that reproductive rights are necessary for improving women's reproductive health.

      This book presents an empirical model of reproductive rights in developing countries. The model encompasses three explanations of reproductive rights. The first explanation proposes that reproductive rights levels are negatively related to population growth. The second explanation argues that gender equality has a positive effect on reproductive rights. Finally we propose that women's education has a positive effect on reproductive rights. The empirical model takes into account the effects of modernization, secularization, and family planning program effort on population growth, women's education, and gender equality.

      The idea that as men and women share power and resources equally, women are more likely to enjoy reproductive rights has for long been the cornerstone of development programs targeted at women. This is also the theoretical basis for the current popularity of women's empowerment programs as a strategy to improve the quality of life among women. Programs, activities, and policies to increase women's reproductive rights are well ahead of empirical research in the area of reproductive rights. This book contributes to empirical reproductive rights research.

Data on one hundred and one developing countries are analyzed using structural equation analysis. Our research findings suggest that value-based structural changes play an important role in improving reproductive rights. The question is, how do we change values. We offer suggestions based on our findings and a few speculations. We have suggested a number of policy directives based on our findings using cross-national data. This study provides a direction for empirical research in the area of reproductive rights.

Acknowledgements

We wish to express our thanks to Fred Pampel at the University of Colorado - Boulder; Joseph Chamie at the United Nations; Cora Martin at the University of North Texas; Lyle Shannon at the University of Iowa; Jay Weinstein at the Eastern Michigan State University; Elizabeth Esterchild at the University of North Texas; Satoshi Kanozawa at the University of Illinois at Urbana; and Paulina Khumba at Wiley College for their constructive comments. We are highly indebted to the Department of Sociology at the University of North Texas and the Department of Sociology and Anthropology at the University of Arkansas at Little Rock for their support. We are deeply indebted to Felicia LeClare at the University of Notre Dame who provided us with extensive commentaries on an earlier version of this book. We would like to extend our thanks to graduate assistant, T.S. Sunil, for his competent assistance throughout the course of this project. This book incorporates several key findings from articles which are to appear in *Social Science Journal, Michigan Sociological Review, International Journal of Comparative Sociology*, and *Canadian Journal of Sociology*. We thank the publishers of these journals for giving us permission to use substantive material from our articles.

1 Introduction

Perhaps one of the most publicized political and social issues of this decade is the issue of women's reproductive rights. A number of social and political phenomena have played a catalytic role in the emergence and current visibility of women's reproductive rights. The most noteworthy among them is the political prominence of humans rights groups and organizations. Since the establishment of the U.N. Commission on the Status of Women (CSW) in 1946, the international community has adopted treaties and recommendations to promote women's rights in political, economic, civil, and social fields. It was not until the recent decades that the right to make reproductive decisions was recognized as a fundamental human right. The population control movements in some developing countries have contributed to the current visibility of women's reproductive rights as a social issue. Reproductive rights include the rights such as the right to decide on the starting, spacing, and stopping of fertility. The basic right to decide on the spacing and number of children may not be taken for granted universally even today. The control over resources to make these reproductive decisions is a key aspect of reproductive rights.

The population control movement is characterized by an emphasis on achieving demographic targets. These targets are often aimed at an improvement in two quantifiable ends: the number of potential births averted and the number of contraceptive users. The strategies for achieving these targets in some developing countries have resulted in numerous violations of women's individual rights and have compromised women's health (Correa, 1994). Family planning programs in Puerto Rico between 1950 and 1970 sterilized without their knowledge a large number of poor women who could not afford private medical care. Mass protests from women against this program led to its abandonment (Correa, 1994).

Birth control programs in developing countries have spawned two major issues: one concerned with the violation of human rights, in particular women's reproductive rights, and the other with an increase in reproductive health risks. The public reaction against an increase in reproductive health risks and violation of rights has been channeled through women's organizations. These organizations have publicized reproductive rights issues in order to bring about improvements in women's reproductive rights.

The growing relevance of reproductive rights in the designing of social service delivery systems has raised controversies. In the main, two conflicting approaches toward providing services, specifically birth control services, have emerged. One is based on the belief that birth control services should be grounded on enabling women to achieve voluntary fertility control. The other approach considers voluntary fertility as a relative concept. The absolute right to have as many children as a woman desires is hardly applicable to poor countries, where the levels of socioeconomic development do not provide resources necessary for women to negotiate rights, at least in the short run.

The two approaches to reproductive rights have spurred human rights debates at international conferences and conventions such as the Vienna conference (the 1993 World Conference on Human Rights) and the Cairo conference (the 1994 International Conference on Population and Development). Despite the lack of agreement on how to secure and promote reproductive rights, the Fourth World Conference on Women held in September 1995 in Beijing defined women's reproductive rights as the right to decide freely and responsibly on the number and spacing of their children free from political and religious persecution. Women's reproductive rights also include the right to have control over their sexuality and reproductive behavior.

Another source of support for reproductive rights stems from the current programs and policies of the women's health movement, specifically as related to reproductive health. The international women's health movement which started in the late 1970s has called into question several features of current population control programs. The international women's health movement challenges the notion that individual well-being may be compromised for the larger goal of attaining population control. In addition, the health movement has questioned social policies that have failed to promote women's reproductive health. Reproductive health is defined as a state of complete well-being with respect to having a safe and satisfying sex life. Reproductive rights are an important aspect of reproductive health. These rights provide women and men the ability to decide the number and timing of births, as well as the access to services necessary to implement fertility decisions. Women's ability to make and implement decisions is a crucial determinant of their health.

At the core of the women's health movement is the claim that every woman has the right to have control over her body, her sexuality, and her reproductive life. DAWN (Development Alternatives with Women for a New

Era), an advocacy agency, speaks for women:

> Control over reproduction is a basic need and a basic right for all women. Linked as it is to women's health and social status, as well as the powerful social structures of religion, state control and administrative inertia, and private profit, it is from the perspective of poor women that this right can best be understood and affirmed. (Sen and Grown, 1987, p.49)

The presence of the three ideologies and practices; family planning, human rights, and women's health, clearly have implications for women's reproductive rights. The proponents of these ideologies seek an empirical understanding of the social and structural basis of women's reproductive rights. The goal of the study is to investigate the social-structural determinants of the levels of women's reproductive rights in developing countries at the nation-state level.

Human Rights, Women's Rights, and Reproductive Rights

International human rights is the first universal ideology (Weissbrodt, 1988). Human rights refer to a loosely organized set of formal and informal rules, codes, and norms which protect individuals against groups and organizations that threaten the survival and dignity of persons. Human rights are universal in scope and also transcend the political tendency to limit the enjoyment of rights based on ascriptive and achieved criteria such as gender, race, and social class. These rights are based on the notion that all human beings are equal and therefore have an equal right to enjoy dignity and security. Rights and freedoms are seen as indivisible. That is, some rights cannot be suppressed in order to promote other rights. A human rights agenda provides the foundation for respecting minority status and ethnic and cultural diversity, and it reinforces the obligations every person has to create a humane physical and social environment for the current as well as future generations of citizens. Rights form the foundation for social action, policy, and reform.

In developing countries, threats against personal security, human rights, and dignity stem from fast changes in social, economic, and political institutions left behind by long periods of European colonization. Almost all developing countries occupy a peripheral role in the modern world economic system. The exploitation of workers on the periphery, particularly women and children, by the core countries worsens the situation of the poor and disadvantaged. In addition, deep social inequalities resulting from marketization and globalization of economies have created a new class of economically and politically powerful elites. This increases the vulnerability of the poor and the powerless in the hands of the elites in developing countries, resulting in an increase in human rights violations. Given the widespread prevalence of authoritarian regimes, socioeconomic inequality, and ethnic conflicts in the developing countries, rights such as the right to life, right to democracy, right to ethnic identity, right to social justice, and the rights of vulnerable groups have become dispensable. The concern about human rights violations has been brought to global attention through several international conventions on human rights. The international vision of human rights has been codified in a number of documents such as the Universal Declaration of Human Rights, the International Covenant on Economic, Social and Cultural Rights, and other United Nations declarations. These declarations describe the scope and meaning of a few fundamental rights.

Among the most vulnerable groups in developing countries are women, children, workers and peasants, disabled persons, and political prisoners. Perhaps one of the most conspicuous social categories which has been historically and universally discriminated against is women. Charlesworth (1995) argues that human rights are inherently biased against women. This is due to the fact that human rights are defined, targeted, and implemented for those who participate in the public spheres of the society and the economy. The discrimination and mistreatment that women suffer in the private sphere, at the family level, are not considered appropriate for intervention by human rights groups and activists.

Charlesworth (1995) points out that women as a group have in many respects been excluded in the discourses of the three generations of human rights. The first generation of rights lays emphasis on civil and political rights. These rights protect men. In particular, in developing countries, the political participation of women is very low. Women's low status in developing countries posses a serious risk to the enjoyment of rights and well-being because resource allocations within the family favor sons and elderly males.

The second generation of rights includes economic, social, and cultural rights. These rights guarantee equal pay for equal work for both men and women. The definition of work, however, does not include the work women do at home. This renders the second generation of rights essentially meaningless for women.

The third generation of rights focuses on group rights. These rights protect the rights of groups. Economic development in developing countries has to an extent eroded the status of women in the public sphere (Hartmann, 1987). This has led to the invisibility of women as a social group. The deterioration that women have faced in their health, educational, and economic status has neither been adequately addressed nor made a focus of concern by human rights declarations (Charlesworth, 1995).

The primary basis for women's rights rests on the fact that women are treated universally different from men. Women are at risk because they are women. The specific social and economic conditions that lead to gender-related risks have not been adequately addressed by current human rights declarations. The social stigma attached to rape in some developing countries keeps raped women from reporting rape. In many developing countries women do not enjoy the same legal status as men. Women are at risk in custody; they are very likely to be raped. Women are more likely to receive harsh punishments for status offenses than men.

The lower status of women within the family is a primary cause of widespread public apathy toward granting equal rights for women and men. Within the household the ability to make fertility decisions affects other rights such as, the right to use contraceptives. More recently, these very gender-related vulnerabilities that women suffer in general have drawn international attention.

The 1993 United Nations Conference on Human Rights held in Vienna marked a turning point in the struggle for women's rights. The effort to divert attention to women's rights bore results when the conference addressed women's rights agendas as a related yet separate aspect of human rights. Women's rights are based on the view that a large share of human rights is essentially women's rights. Thus, the women's rights movement is characterized as a civil rights movement. Consider violence against women and birth control. Issues such as violence against women and the freedom to use birth control have long been considered family issues to be resolved by either family members or social workers. These problems have historically been addressed by women's organizations locally and regionally.

The forcing of this issue to an international level as an integral aspect of women's ability to preserve bodily integrity is an important achievement. Human rights are no longer seen merely as those issues that can effectively be controlled by the state using its police and military powers. International agencies and the state now bear the responsibilities to address women's rights and to ensure women citizens protection from oppression and injustice originating from gender discrimination and social inequalities. The women's rights movement has been able to reshape thinking about human rights, specifically in that human rights may not be divorced from the primary institution of the family.

The Fourth World Conference on Women held in Beijing in 1995 is among the most recent efforts at addressing women's rights as human rights. The conference concluded with hard-hitting recommendations advocating sexual freedom and denouncing violence against women.

The major recommendations made by the conferences are as follows: a) women have the right to decide freely all matters related to sexuality and childbearing; b) the systematic rape of women in wartime is a crime and must be immediately stopped; c) children have the right to privacy when receiving health information, and children's rights must be viewed against parental rights; d) the representation of women in political and economic institutions must increase; e) governments should guarantee women equal rights to inherit, although they may not necessarily inherit the same amount as sons in every instance; f) within the family women should not suffer discrimination because they are mothers; and g) marital rape, genital mutilation of girls, domestic battering, and sexual harassment at work must be considered as human rights violations. These recommendations are broad-based and include measures to protect women's reproductive rights.

The first formal declaration of reproductive rights took place at the 1968 United Nations International Conference on Human Rights in Teheran, Iran. Reproductive rights were defined as the rights of parents to decide freely and responsibly on the number and spacing of children and the right to access and consume information and social services necessary to implement reproductive decisions. The World Population Plan of Action adopted in Bucharest six years later reaffirmed the right of couples and individuals to reproductive decision making.

> All couples and individuals have the basic right to decide freely and responsibly the number and spacing of their children and to have the information, education and means to do so; the responsibility of couples and individuals in the exercise of this right takes into account the needs of their living and future children, and their responsibilities toward the community. (United Nations, 1974)

The International Conference on Population and Development held in Cairo in 1994 and the 1995 Beijing Conference on Women upheld the view that reproductive rights are human rights to be respected and guarded cross-nationally despite religious and cultural differences (Correa and Petchesky,

1994). Reproductive rights are defined as the rights of couples and individuals to decide freely and responsibly the number and spacing of their children, the right to be educated and informed in this matter, and the right to have control over their bodies. The definition of reproductive rights is broad-based in two respects. First, rights belong to all couples and individuals. Second, rights extend to all aspects, including those of control over bodies. Appendix A presents the chronology of the definitions of reproductive rights as adopted by world conferences and conventions during the last three decades.

The Objectives of the Study

This book examines the social-structural influences on the levels of women's reproductive rights. Using data from 101 developing countries,[1] we test a causal model of reproductive rights.

This study attempts to lay a foundation for a sociological approach toward understanding the phenomenon of reproductive rights cross-nationally. The scope is limited to a cross-national analysis of developing countries. This decision was made because developed countries, mostly Western nations, share several socioeconomic and political characteristics, such as the presence of stable democracies and capitalistic market economies. The social, economic, and political context in which women's rights are realized in developed nations differs widely from the social, economic, and political characteristics of developing nations.

Ongoing debates on women's reproductive rights heighten the need for empirical research and theoretical explanations. Few studies have tested a causal model of women's reproductive rights. Sjoberg and Vaughan (1993) state that American sociologists have ignored the issue of rights, which has far-reaching cross-national and cross-cultural significance. This is a field in which sociologists are well equipped to make theoretical and empirical contributions.

Since the 1960s, there has been little research on the relationship between law, and social organizations, and social policies (Black, 1976; Benda-Beckmann, 1989; Simon and Lynch, 1989). Sociologists have seldom examined the role that social-structural factors play in determining the levels of reproductive rights in developing countries. Rights are institutionalized as legal norms. Sociologists often use norms to explain social phenomena. Normative attributes are treated as preconditions. Turner (1993) states that sociologists in general have ignored the issue of rights.

Several developing countries are currently attempting to develop policies and programs related to women's reproductive health. An understanding of the social and economic correlates of reproductive rights is necessary to formulate sound policies for reproductive health programs. In fact, the level of reproductive health in developing countries is low. The various sources of risks which threaten the enjoyment of reproductive health in developing countries remain obscure. However, it is not known that the common sources of these risks lie in societal factors, such as lack of conjugal power among women, illiteracy, and low levels of social and economic development (United Nations, 1996). The extent of reproductive illness among women in developing countries today is indicative of the low levels of reproductive rights among women. The need to address the issue of reproductive rights in developing countries is immediate and pressing. This is evident from a cursory survey of the reproductive health problems that women face on a daily basis in developing countries.

The social forces which mold the reproductive rights movement today broadly stem from three related sources. Women's health and population control movements have generated several policy-oriented issues with regard to targets and strategies which influence individual-level outcomes related to reproductive well-being. The third is the value system that has developed globally around human rights. Historically, conditions which increase the vulnerability of social groups to risks of death and large-scale social and economic exploitations have triggered societal responses. These responses have often been geared toward minimizing the consequences of injury and decreasing the vulnerability through preventive political and legal measures. Thus, the rise of human rights values in many instances motivates state actions in terms of policy measures to improve social and economic rights. Investigation of reproductive rights necessitates a discussion of the two sources of influence, namely, the development of human rights values and the direct and indirect state policies such as population control policies.

The second chapter discusses state policies which have directly or indirectly influenced reproductive rights are presented. In the third chapter, we present the evolution of rights as a concept. In addition, an account of international conferences which have contributed to values and value changes related to reproductive rights is presented. Chapter 4 presents the influences of women's health movements on reproductive rights. Chapter 5 introduces classical and contemporary social theoretical perspectives on rights. Chapter 6

Introduction 9

discusses the three explanations of reproductive rights which we have proposed. The research design for testing the proposed explanations is in chapter 7. Chapter 8 presents the results of the empirical tests of the reproductive rights explanations. Chapter 9 tests post hoc models of women's reproductive rights. This is an attempt to gain some insight into the phenomenon of reproductive rights by utilizing the information from the data we use for testing the proposed model of reproductive rights. Chapter 10 presents discussion and conclusion.

Note

1. One hundred and two countries are identified by the World Bank (1994a) as developing countries: 39, in Sub-Saharan Africa; 24, Latin America/Caribbean; 16, in Middle East/North Africa; and 23, in Asia. Due to data unavailability, Taiwan has been dropped from the study.

Sub-Saharan Africa: Angola, Benin, Botswana, Burkina Faso, Burundi, Cameroon, Central African Republic, Chad, Congo, Cote d' Ivoire, Ethiopia, Gabon, Ghana, Guinea, Guinea Bissau, Kenya, Lesotho, Liberia, Madagascar, Malawi, Mali, Mauritania, Mauritius, Mozambique, Namibia, Niger, Nigeria, Rwanda, Senegal, Sierra Leone, Somalia, South Africa, Sudan, Tanzania, Togo, Uganda, Zaire, Zambia, Zimbabwe.

Latin America/Caribbean: Argentina, Bolivia, Brazil, Chile, Columbia, Costa Rica, Cuba, Dominican Republic, Ecuador, El Salvador, Guatemala, Guyana, Haiti, Honduras, Jamaica, Mexico, Nicaragua, Panama, Paraguay, Peru, Puerto Rico, Trinidad and Tobago, Uruguay, Venezuela.

Middle East/North Africa: Algeria, Egypt, Iran, Iraq, Jordan, Kuwait, Lebanon, Libya, Morocco, Oman, Saudi Arabia, Syria, Tunisia, Turkey, United Arab Emirates, Yemen,

Asia: Afghanistan, Bangladesh, Bhutan, Cambodia, China, Hongkong, India, Indonesia, Korea (Democratic), Korea (Republic), Laos, Malaysia, Mongolia, Myanmar (Burma), Nepal, Pakistan, Papua New Guinea, Philippines, Singapore, Sri Lanka, Thailand, Vietnam.

2 State Population Control Policies and Reproductive Rights

World population in 1990 was about 5.3 billion. Approximately 77 percent of this population lived in developing countries (World Resources Institute, 1992). According to the United Nations' population projections, world population will be 8.6 billion by the year 2025 if death rates remain constant (United Nations, 1996). Large-scale population increases will occur in poor countries of Africa, where the population is projected to nearly triple between 1990 and 2025. The population gap between developing and developed countries will thus be widened. About 84 percent of the world population will be living in developing countries by the year 2025 (World Resources Institute, 1992).

When the international community gathered in Teheran in 1968, there was a widespread consensus that overpopulation, especially in developing countries, contributes to international conflicts. If unchecked, the conference claimed, population growth will present a potentially insurmountable obstacle to socioeconomic development and to the enjoyment of a wide range of human rights. A quarter of a century later, the same belief prevailed at the 1994 Cairo conference, which concluded that spiraling population growth in developing countries has been eating away the fruits of development efforts.

The concept of "overpopulation" carries with it fearful images of teeming cities with starving people, desperate women with hungry children, massive environmental degradation with overcrowded slums, and large-scale abuses of human rights. "The population bomb threatens to create an explosion as disruptive and dangerous as an explosion of the atom, and with as much influence on prospects for progress or disaster, war or peace" (Greissimer, 1954, p. 40). Freedman and Isaacs (1993) warn, "the grim scenarios of global devastation are beginning to fill the air" (p. 21). Overpopulation has caused human destitution and misery. High rates of population growth are seen as monumental barriers to the achievement of reproductive rights and women's rights in general. The idea that high rates of population growth are inimical to development underlies most population control programs and policies. The development approach to curbing population growth is based on the belief that people will voluntarily limit family size when they perceive opportunities for social mobility. Economic development is a necessary precondition for social mobility. This approach espoused by the so-called developmentalists focuses solely on economic gains from low population growth rates. Improvement in per capita availability of social and health services, women's labor force participation, and standard of living are seen as desirable outcomes. This emphasis on micro-level outcomes neglects women's social status and rights at the family level. The reinforcement of patriarchal structures resulting from development processes also erodes women's decision-making powers. This consequence of development is often overlooked.

The international conferences on world population held in Bucharest (1974), Mexico City (1984), and Cairo (1994), despite some widely divergent viewpoints, reached a consensus on the necessity to control population growth in developing countries. The preamble of the Program of Action adopted at the 1994 Cairo conference states that the conference represents "the last opportunity in the 20th century to collectively address the critical challenges and interrelationships between population and development" (p.8). The preamble of the Program of Action of the United Nations International Conference on Population and Development is presented in Appendix B.

> The current objective of population control programs is to curb population growth in developing countries over the next 20 years and to stabilize world population below the estimated 7.5 billion by the year 2025. In a 1986 policy study entitled *Population Growth and Policies in Sub-Saharan Africa*, the World Bank isolated population assistance as the most important economic strategy, especially in Africa, to control unchecked population growth. (World Bank, 1986)

Fertility policies aimed at reducing population size in developing countries have been funded by the United States Agency for International Development (USAID), family planning non-governmental organizations (NGOs), and United Nations agencies such as the United Nations Fund for Population Activities (UNFPA) (until 1986) and the World Bank. The United States government has consistently been the largest donor for population programs (Gillespie and Seltzer, 1990). In 1965, only 21 countries actively supported family planning programs (Isaacs and Cook, 1984). In 1989, 123 countries had active family planning programs covering 91 percent of the world's population (United Nations, 1989).

The availability of a large variety of birth control and organizational technologies has spawned a number of possible strategies for achieving the objective of population control. The harmful effects of technology are a function of the ways technologies are utilized (Hardon, 1992; Meyer and Meyer, 1997). A number of family planning programs have been accused of excessive use of force (Lane, 1994). Family planning programs cross-nationally can be grouped into two categories on the basis of strategies used for the provision of contraceptive services and technologies, the voluntary approach and the involuntary approach.

The voluntary approach rejects the use of coercion for fertility control. This approach proposes that population policies must protect individuals' dignity and freedom to make reproductive decisions. In general, population policies must respect women's rights and freedom.[1] Romania's compulsory gynecological examinations in workplaces and the alleged forced sterilization of Gypsies in Eastern Europe violated the norms of the voluntary approach. The Chinese family planning program has been criticized for its coercive methods of population control.

The involuntary approach compromises the voluntary control of fertility in favor of coercive methods of enforcing fertility control. This approach views reproductive regulations imposed on individuals by the state authority as enabling sustainable development and benefitting future generation(s). The "stewardship" thesis holds that individual welfare cannot be advanced without collective action to limit population size. Li (1993), in defense of the birth control policy in China, identifies a number of factors which necessitate strong state-centered family planning programs. These programs may limit individual-level freedom to make reproductive decisions in the short run. Li (1993) argues that scarce resources, inaccessible health care, and social and cultural pressure in some developing countries constrain women's ability to make reproductive decisions and considerably increase the risk of contracting sexually transmitted diseases. He maintains that defining reproductive rights as absolute freedom from coercion from the state sets an impossible standard unachieveable under current levels of social and economic development in developing countries and will perpetuate discrimination against women (Li, 1993).

Li (1993) maintains that the concept of reproductive rights as defined by Western countries connotes the absence of coercion or state intervention. He argues that this concept is not necessarily applicable to developing societies, including China. The patriarchal family system and economic conditions in those countries fail to provide women with sufficient control over their bodies and reproductive decision-making. Theories of rights in Western discourse have generally not paid sufficient attention to the severity of such oppression in developing nations (Li, 1993).

> Only when social and economic conditions necessary to enable women to protect their basic right to reproductive health are achieved, can women of those countries make responsible reproductive choices... A concept of reproductive rights that focused solely on freedom from coercion would provide little impetus or justification for efforts to create those conditions. (Li, 1993, pp. 6-7)

The involuntary approach or the stewardship approach suggests that unrestricted population growth is a hindrance to social and economic development and that it is the state's responsibility to control population size for the good of the public and future generation(s). The principal argument of the involuntary perspective is that reproductive rights, if understood as individual liberties, are meaningless since they cannot be realized in poor countries where enabling conditions of social welfare, personal security, and political freedom do not exist (Correa, 1994).

The two approaches share the belief that overpopulation hinders socioeconomic development and that contraceptive techniques and family planning programs provide an effective means to control population growth. But the voluntary and involuntary approaches differ in their strategies to limit population size. The voluntary approach attempts to advance individual well-being without government intervention. Government policies create and maintain structural apparatuses necessary for delivering contraceptive services, health services, and public information services on the basis of the respect for individual decision-making (Anand, 1994). This freedom to exercise individual reproductive choices regardless of societal conditions, such as economic development level, is taken for granted.

The stewardship approach, however, believes that too much emphasis on individual freedom in reproductive decision-making during the early stages of economic development is not desirable. Reproductive rights are to be granted when social and economic conditions make reproductive rights relevant and meaningful for the enjoyment of reproductive life.

Note

1. Sen (1991) provided an example of well-being and freedom. One person starved to death out of choice because of her/his religious beliefs. The other died of hunger because she/he was very poor and lacked the means to command food. Even though both persons achieved the same level of well-being, the first person's well-being freedom is greater than the second person's.

3   Value Systems and Reproductive Rights

This chapter is divided into two sections. The first section describes the evolution of the concept of rights and provides an analysis of the values related to reproductive rights. The second section chronicles selected international conferences and conventions on human rights, women's rights, and reproductive rights.

The Evolution of Rights

The philosophical basis for rights remains a matter of disagreement. For some, reproductive rights are natural rights. For others, reproductive rights are socially determined entitlement that requires state intervention to address social inequalities (Petchesky, 1990). The origin of the term *rights* can be traced to the idea of "inalienable" rights in the 17th and 18th century England. Theories about individual liberties underlying the French and American revolutions paved the way for later thoughts on economic and social rights.

Rights as Natural Rights and Individual Liberty

The idea of the rights of individuals originated from early philosophical, sociological, and legal propositions on natural law and natural rights, which suggest that individuals are entitled to certain immutable rights. The European liberal thought assumes that the state is a threat rather than a help when it comes to the exercise of rights (de Laubier, 1985). The spirit of the 17th and 18th century Western thought is embodied in the English Bill of Rights of 1689, the American Bill of Rights of 1789, and the Declaration of Rights of Man and of the Citizen adopted by the French National Assembly in 1789.

The 18th-century Enlightenment tradition holds that human beings are rational beings and are entitled to certain rights. During the late 18th and early

19th centuries, governments began to recognize the inherent rights of individuals in their national laws. The American Declaration of Independence of 1776 proclaimed the inalienable rights to life, liberty, and the pursuit of happiness. These rights followed from the 18th century European philosophical assumption that individuals are autonomous in nature. In 1789 the French Revolution produced the Declaration of the Rights of Man and of Citizens. The United States and French constitutions were to an extent replicated by the written constitutions of the Netherlands (1798), Sweden (1809), Spain (1812), Norway (1814), Belgium (1831), Liberia (1847), Sardinia (1848), Denmark (1849), and Prussia (1850). The concept of reproductive rights as inalienable individual rights is ideologically embedded in the notion that all individuals have the rights to enjoy freedom and happiness. The assumption that individuals are autonomous, self-containing, and self-determining is the by-product of the growth of the civil society in Western nations.

Rights as Social Entitlement

The development of socialism in the 19th century expanded the concept of rights as natural rights to include not only the right to be free from state intervention, but also the right to have the state redress economic inequality. The socialist model sought to extend equality in the social sphere rather than in individual sphere (de Laubier, 1985). The theory of individual rights as social entitlement emphasizes the responsibility of the state to guarantee the freedom of opportunities to its citizens. More importantly, the state also guarantees that all persons are assured of certain entitlements (Dixon-Mueller, 1993). These entitlements are often called economic and social rights, or *welfare rights*, as distinct from civil and political rights. As set forth in the Universal Declaration (see Appendix C), these rights include the rights to an adequate standard of living, to education, to work, to just and favorable conditions of work, and to protection against unemployment. These rights and freedoms are intended to apply to everyone "without distinction of any kind, such as race, color, sex, language, religion, political or other opinion, national or social origin, property, birth or other status" and without regard to the "political, jurisdictional or international status of the country or territory to which a person belongs" (United Nations, 1973, p.1).

The transition from individual liberty to social entitlement brings with it certain obligations on the part of the citizens. For example, the right to health is accompanied by an obligation to vaccinate one's children against certain infectious diseases, and the right to education is followed by a moral obligation for parents to send children of a certain age to school (de Laubier, 1985).

Simon Vei (1978), France's former minister of health, remarks that we have arrived at a curious reversal of things. He observes that out of liberty is born obligation, and the exercise of a right is rendered essentially compulsory.

The philosophical and social origins of rights in the developing countries differ from those of developed nations. These concepts diffused to the developing countries during the period of colonization. The current recognition and sharing of Western ideals of rights in developing countries is in part due to their membership in global entities such as the United Nations.

Rights in Social Movements, International Conferences, and Conventions

Attention to the issue of rights began to develop in the 16th and 18th centuries. During this early period the focus was on the protection of religious minorities. Military interventions sought to punish states that were found guilty of abusing minority populations.

The 19th century effort to abolish slave trade and to protect the rights of workers marked a growing international concern for human rights. Slavery had existed in most regions of the world for centuries, but it was not until the 19th century that collective international measures were taken to eradicate slavery and the slave trade (Weissbrodt, 1988).

The ideology of human rights grew significantly in the years following World War I, which claimed 20 million lives. A selected list of international organizations on human rights is presented in Appendix D. The International Committee of the Red Cross (ICRC) was founded at the 1869 Geneva International Conference for the purpose of reducing the horror of war. The horror over World War I led to the formation in 1919 of the League of Nations. The League was based on Enlightenment ideas of natural reason. Human rights concerns also led to the establishment of the International Labor Organization (ILO) in 1919.[1] The ILO came into being with the dissolution of the old international order at the end of World War I and remained as a free-standing international organization after the collapse of the League of Nations.

The 19th century saw the beginning of the codification of instruments for the protection of the victims of war and for restraints on the methods and means of warfare. Opposition to the slave trade continued throughout the 19th century and was codified in 1929 at the proceedings of the League of Nations Convention to Suppress the Slave Trade and Slavery. The 1956 Supplementary Convention on the Abolition of Slavery, the Slave Trade and Institutions and Practices Similar to Slavery expanded the scope of the 1926 Convention on the Condemnation of Slavery and Servitude.

The United Nations Charter adopted in 1945 was the first international treaty to enunciate the principle of human rights in specific terms. The Charter placed international human rights within the context of international law. It reaffirmed the mission of the United Nations as promoting and encouraging the respect for human rights and fundamental freedom for all, without distinction as to race, sex, language or religion. Article 1 of the Charter defined the purposes of the United Nations as follows:

> 1. To maintain international peace and security.
> 2. To develop friendly relations among nations based on respect for the principle of equal rights and self-determination of peoples, and to take other appropriate measures to strengthen universal peace.
> 3. To achieve international cooperation in solving international problems of an economic, social, cultural, or humanitarian character, and in promoting and encouraging respect for human rights and for fundamental freedoms for all without distinction as to race, sex, language, or religion.
> 4. To be a center for harmonizing the actions of nations in the attainment of these common ends.

In response to the issue of human rights after the second World War, the four Geneva conventions of 1949 supplemented the Geneva convention of 1864. The first three conventions provided for the treatment of the sick and the wounded members of the armed forces in the field and at sea and the treatment of prisoners of war. The fourth Geneva convention extended to the protection of the civilians in time of war.

The Universal Declaration on Human Rights (Bill of Rights), adopted in 1948 with no dissenting votes, provided the most authoritative definition of the rights and obligations. The central theme of the declaration is the principle of equality and non-discrimination. It endorsed the fundamental human rights to have the security of life and liberty, equality before law; freedom from arbitrary interference with privacy, family, and home. In addition, the declaration sought to promote rights to social security; realization of economic, social, and cultural rights indispensable for dignity; and free development of personality. The extension of these rights enveloped the spheres of work, rest, leisure, and education, including the prior right of parents to choose the kind of education to be given to their children.

> All human beings are born free and equal in dignity and rights (Article 1).
> Everyone is entitled to all the rights and freedoms set forth in this Declaration, without distinction of any kind, such as race, color, sex, language, religion, political or other opnion, national or social origin, property, birth or other status (Article 2).
> Everyone has the right to life, liberty and security of person (Article 3).
> Everyone has the right to recognition everywhere as a person before the law (Article 6).
> 1. Men and women of full age, without any limitation due to race, nationality or religion, have the right to marry and to found a family. They are entitled to equal rights as to marriage, during marriage and at its dissolution.
> 2. Marriage shall be entered into only with the free and full consent of the intending spouses.
> 3. The family is the natural and fundamental group unit of society and is entitled to protection by society and the State (Article 16).
> 1. Everyone has the right to standard of living adequate for the health and well-being of himself and of his family, including food, clothing, housing and medical care and necessary social services, and the right to security in the event of unemployment, sickness, disability, widowhood, old age or other lack of livelihood in circumstances beyond his control.
> 2. Motherhood and childhood are entitled to special care and assistance...
> (Article 25)

In order to implement the Universal Declaration of Human Rights and to translate the original principles in the Declaration into treaty provisions, two multilateral conventions were drafted by the Human Rights Committee in 1954 and approved by the General Assembly of the United Nations in 1966, one on civil and political rights, the other on social and economic rights. The International Covenant on Civil and Political Rights encompassed most of the rights specified in the Bill of Rights and furthermore provided for the right to self-determination. Article 1 states that:

> all people have the right of self-determination. By virtue of that right they freely determine their political status and freely pursue their economic, social and cultural development.
> The States Parties to the present Covenant, including those having responsibility for the administration of Non-Self-Governing and Trust Territories, shall promote the realization of the right of self-determination,

and shall respect that right, in conformity with the provisions of the Charter of the United Nations.

The Covenant contained the right to the dispose of property, the right to nationality at birth, the right to move freely within a country, and the right to leave a country. Article 6 states that "every human being has the inherent right to life. This right shall be protected by law. No one shall be arbitrarily deprived of his life."

The International Covenant on Economic, Social, and Cultural Rights is a charter of basic rights in economic, social, and cultural areas. The Covenant recognized the right to work, just and favorable conditions of work, the right to social security, the right of everyone to an adequate standard of living, the right to the highest attainable standard of physical and mental health, the right of everyone to an education, the right of every one to take part in the cultural life, to enjoy the benefits of scientific progress and its application, and to benefit from any scientific, literary, or artistic production of which he/she is the author. The Covenant further recognized that marriage must be entered into with the free consent of the intending spouses, that special protection should be accorded to mothers, and that special measures of protection and assistance should be taken on behalf of children. The International Covenant on Economic, Social, and Cultural Rights required that ratifying nations ensure fair wages and equal remuneration for equal work, equal promotional opportunities, safe and healthful working conditions, rest, leisure and reasonable limitation of working hours, the right to form and join trade unions, the right of trade unions to function freely, and the right to strike. It called on ratifying nations to take measures to improve methods of production, conservation, and distribution of food, to reduce stillbirths and infant mortality, to improve environmental and industrial hygiene, to prevent and control diseases, to assure the availability of medical care to all, and to make primary education compulsory and secondary and higher education generally available and equally accessible to all.

Two of the early population documents that address the relationship between population growth and individual human rights are the World Population Plan of Action (WPPA), adopted at the World Population Conference (1974), and, the Recommendations for the Further Implementation of the Plan of Action adopted at the 1984 International Conference on Population. John D. Rockefeller III, in his speech at the World Population Conference 1974, argued that the population field had moved in directions that jeopardized its central concern with human well-being.

The basis of my interest from the first has been the individual, not his or her relationship to some demographic tabulation, important as it is. To me, interest in population means interest in the problems, well-being and future of people. There are four elements of reappraisal which I believe are essential to the attainment of effective results.
The first is the relationship between population policy and economic and social development...
The second ... is the need to revise our concept of economic growth... Whether in the industrial nations or the developing nations, growth should be pursued not for its own sake, but to meet basic human needs for jobs, food, shelter, health, education.
The third key element of reappraisal is active recognition of the growing interdependence of all peoples and nations. In an interdependent world, the internal task of the developed nations is clear – to stabilize their own populations and moderate their levels of consumption in a sensible and orderly way.
The final element ... is the role of women in society... new and urgent attention to the role of women must be a vital characteristic of any modern development program... In my opinion, if we are to make genuine progress in economic and social development, if we are to make progress in achieving population goals, women increasingly must have greater freedom of choice in determining their roles in society. (Boland et al; 1994, p. 92)

Beginning in the 19th century, liberal reformers and radical utopians proposed that human rights be extended to women, which led to women's emancipation movements. The Commission on the Status of Women (CSW) was established in 1946 as a functional commission of the Economic and Social Council resolution to prepare recommendations and reports to the Council on promoting women's rights in political, economic, civil, social, and educational fields. The objective of the Commission is to promote implementation of the principle that women and men shall have equal rights. In other words, CSW is the global advocate for equality between women and men.

It was not until the 1950s that a number of United Nations documents began to address rights issues specifically concerning women. Correa and Petchesky (1994) argue that women's rights have generally been neglected and that the Bill of Rights has been faulted for lack of gender sensitivity and failure to articulate reproductive rights. The International Labor Organization promulgated a number of conventions that pertain to the rights of women (Defeis, 1991). The Convention Concerning Equal Remuneration for Men and Women Workers for Work of Equal Value of the International Labor Organization (1951) defined the term "equal remuneration for men and women workers for work of equal value" as the "rates of remuneration established without discrimination based on sex" (Article 1). Article 2 specified that "each Member shall, by means appropriate to the methods in operation for determining rates of remuneration, promote and, in so far as is consistent with such methods, ensure the application to all workers of the principle of equal remuneration for men and women for work of equal value" (p. 1).

The Convention Concerning Discrimination (Employment and Occupation) was convened in 1958. The Convention defined discrimination as including "any distinction, exclusion or preference made on the basis of race, color, sex, religion, political opinion, national extraction or social origin, which has the effect of nullifying or impairing equality of opportunity or treatment in employment or occupation as may be determined by the member concerned after consultation with representative employers' and workers' organizations, and with other appropriate bodies", "and in respect of a particular job based on the inherent requirements thereof shall not be deemed to be discrimination"(Article 1).

The Convention Concerning Employment Promotion and Protection against Unemployment of the International Labor Organization was convened in 1988 and entered into force in 1991. The general provisions of the convention declared that "each member shall ensure equality of treatment for all persons protected, without discrimination on the basis of race, color, sex, religion, political opinion, national extraction, nationality ethic or social origin, disability or age" (Article 6). The convention required member states to aim at ensuring "inter alia" (Article 7). Article 8 specified that "each member shall endeavor to establish, subject to national law and practice, special program to promote additional job opportunities and employment assistance and to encourage freely chosen and productive employment for identified categories of disadvantaged persons having or liable to have difficulties in finding lasting employment such as women, young workers, disabled persons, older workers, the long-term unemployed, migrant workers lawfully resident in the country and workers affected by structural change."

The Convention on Political Rights of Women, the Convention on the Consent to Marriage, Minimum Age for Marriage and Registration of Marriage, and the Convention on Nationality of Married Women directly addressed issues related to the status of women. The convention on Political Rights of Women entered into force in July 1954. The Convention recognized that everyone has the right to take part in the government of his or her country directly or indirectly through freely chosen representatives, to have equal access to public service in one's country, and to the enjoyment and exercise of political rights. Article 1 of the convention specified that "women shall be entitled to vote in all elections on equal terms with men, without any discrimination." The convention proclaimed that women should be eligible to serve in all publicly elected bodies and entitled to hold public office and to exercise all public functions without any discrimination. The convention on the Consent to Marriage, Minimum Age for Marriage and Registration of Marriage entered into force in December 1964. It reaffirmed that all marriages must be based on the full and free consent of both parties and that no marriage can be entered into by any person under the legally specified minimum age. The Convention on Nationality of Married Women entered into force in August 1958. The convention required that the celebration or dissolution of marriage will not affect the nationality of the wife (see Article 1) and that the voluntary acquisition of another state or renunciation of its nationality by one of its nationals will not prevent the retention of its nationality by the wife of such national (see Article 2).

The Declaration on the Elimination of All Forms of Discrimination against Women (1967) proclaimed that preventing women's participation in political, social, economic, and cultural life on equal terms with men is an obstacle to the full development of the potentials of women in the services of their countries and humanity.

> Article1: Discrimination against women, denying or limiting as it does their equality of rights with men, is fundamentally unjust and contributes an offence against human dignity.

The declaration called for appropriate measures to ensure the same rights of women with men in all fields of life.

In 1972 the United Nations Assembly adopted a resolution and proclaimed that 1975, the International Women's Year, be devoted to intensified action to promote equality between men and women, to ensure the full integration of women in the total development effort, and to increase the contribution of women to the strengthening of world peace. In 1975 the General Assembly announced 1976-1985 as the United Nations Decade for Women: Equality, Development, and Peace (Boland et al., 1994).

At the International Women's Year Conference held in 1975 in Mexico, a world plan of action on the equality of women and their contribution to development and peace was adopted. In 1980 the second World Conference of the United Nations Decade for Women was held in Copenhagen, focusing on the themes of women in the decade, employment, health, and education.

The major instrument specifically pertinent to the status of women is the Convention on the Elimination of All Forms of Discrimination against Women (1979) (Appendix E). It is the most comprehensive and detailed international legal instrument to date covering the rights of women. The convention provided a universal definition of discrimination against women. Article 1 defined the term discrimination against women as "any distinction, exclusion or restriction mode on the basis of sex which has the effect or purpose of impairing or nullifying the recognition, enjoyment or exercise by women, irrespective of their marital status, on a basis of equality of men and women, of human rights and fundamental freedoms in the political, economic, social, cultural, civil or any other field." It established rights for women in areas not previously subject to international standards. It is the only international treaty whose provisions address family planning. Article 12 of the convention urged the states parties to "take all appropriate measures to eliminate discrimination against women in the field of health care in order to ensure, on a basis of equality of men and women, access to health care services, including those related to family planning" and to "ensure to women appropriate services in connection with pregnancy, confinement and the post-natal period, granting free services where necessary, as well as adequate nutrition during pregnancy and lactation." By 1996, 154 countries had ratified the Convention.[2]

In June 1993, the World Conference on Human Rights held in Vienna expanded the international human rights agenda to include gender-specific violations. The Vienna Declaration and Program of Action identified gender-specific abuses as human rights violations and called for the integration of women's human rights throughout United Nations activities.

Violence against women is defined by the draft declaration as "any act of gender-based violence that results in, or is likely to result in, physical, sexual or psychological harm or suffering to women, including threats of such acts, coercion or arbitrary deprivation of liberty, whether occurring in public or private life" (Article 1, UN Doc. A/C.3/48/L.5, attachment 3.20 December 1993). Specific forms of violence are identified in Article 2 under the categories of violence in the family, violence within the general community, and violence perpetrated or condoned by the state.[3]

> Violence against women shall be understood to encompass, but not be limited to, the following:
> (a) Physical, sexual and psychological violence occurring in the family, including battering, sexual abuse of female children in the household, dowry-related violence, marital rape, female genital mutilation and other traditional

practices harmful to women, non-spousal violence and violence related to exploitation;

(b) Physical, sexual and psychological violence occurring within the general community, including rape, sexual abuse, sexual harassment and intimidation at work, in educational institutions and elsewhere, trafficking in women and forced prostitution;

(c) Physical, sexual and psychological violence perpetrated or condoned by the State, wherever it occurs. (Article 2)

The conference crystallized a political consensus that various forms of violence against women should be examined in conjunction with gender discrimination and within the context of human rights standards. The link between women's subordinate status in society and gender-based violence was discussed, both at the regional preparatory meetings and at the conference. The declaration asserts that women's human rights are an inalienable, integral, and indivisible part of universal human rights.

In July 1985, the Third Conference on Women was held in Nairobi. The Nairobi Forward-looking Strategies for the Advancement of Women was adopted to review and appraise the achievements of the decade for women and to develop strategies for overcoming the obstacles still remaining. Women all over the world gathered in the capital city of Beijing, China, in September 1995. The Fourth World Conference on Women called for international effort to strive for socioeconomic and political equalities of women. The Platform for Action reaffirms that the human rights of women and girls are part of universal human rights. The platform recognizes the necessity of broad-based and sustained economic growth in the context of sustainable development for social development and justice, and calls for the adequate mobilization of resources at the national and international levels and new and additional resources from all available funding mechanisms (Chapter 1). The platform identifies that the advancement of women and the achievement of gender equality are matters of human rights and are conditions for social justice. Strategies and actions should give priority to eradicate the feminization of poverty, discrimination in education and health, violence against women, armed conflicts, inequality in women's access to and participation in economic structures and decision making, and insufficient mechanisms at national and international levels for the advancement of women. The conference called for (1) access for women to political structures at all levels and equal political empowerment at all decision-making levels; (2) recognition, protection, compensation, financial, and other assistance and full legal status for millions of women and children and the victims of nuclear and other environmental catastrophes, many of them widows or orphans; (3) universally accessible, high quality, non-discriminatory health care, to sponsor and support women controlled research for the prevention and cure of HIV/AIDS, to prohibit any form of discrimination of women with HIV/AIDS, and to ensure women's access to information, care, support, and treatment of HIV/AIDS; (4) the development and sustained use of affirmative action by both the private and public sectors of society to ensure the equality of women; (5) all the media to change the present negative, exploitive, and sexualized images of women and children to positive ones; (6) a reshaping of education for all children, beginning at the primary levels, to sensitize them about human rights, gender issues, and non-violent conflict resolution, stressing the need for world peace; (7) full implementation of the UN Decade for Human Rights Education and the prevention of human rights violations against women; (8) new and additional financial, technical, and other resources to successfully implement the plans and commitments from the Nairobi, Rio de Janeiro, Vienna, Cairo, Copenhagen, and Beijing Conferences and member states to fulfil their obligations under the Convention on the Elimination of All Forms of Discrimination against Women.

Women's social movements and international legislation have contributed to the improvement of women's status in society. However, the rights of women in the area of reproductive decision making are far from being codified.

At the International Conference on Human Rights held in Teheran in 1968, reproductive rights were bestowed on parents and were defined as the right to decide freely and responsibly on the number and spacing of children and the right to gain adequate education and information in this respect. The World Population Plan of Action adopted in Bucharest (1974) reaffirmed the right of reproductive decision making to "all couples and individuals" who have the basic right to decide freely and responsibly the number and spacing of their children and to have the information, education, and means to do so. The responsibility of couples and individuals in the exercise of this right takes into account the needs of their living and future children and their responsibilities toward the community (United Nations, 1974).

The Bucharest declaration differed from the Teheran declaration in several respects. First, it expanded the scope of rights to include "parents" and "couples and individuals." Second, it stated that people should have the means for information and education to assert the rights. Finally, it tried to define the elusive concept of responsible decision making (Freedman and Isaacs, 1993).

The next international conference was held a decade later in Mexico City. The statement of the Mexico City conference on population further defined what "responsibility" means.

> Any recognition of rights also implies responsibilities: in this case, it implies that couples and individuals should exercise this right, taking into consideration their own situation, as well as the implications of their decisions for the balanced development of their children and of the community and society in which they live. (United Nations, 1984, Recommendation 26)

The health approach began to emerge around 1985, when the health field began to focus its increasing attention on women's health for its own sake. The concept of women's reproductive rights as the freedom to decide on the number and spacing of their children and to gain information and education was extended to include the right of women for reproductive health in the last decade or so (Fathalla, 1992). In spite of the abortion controversy at the International Conference on Population and Development (1994), women's reproductive rights were expanded to include the right to have control over their own bodies.

In sum, the current concept of rights defined by international conferences on human rights and population has its origins in the philosophical and ideological traditions of the West. The rapid growth of women's organizations in the 20th century contributed toward forcing women's issues as human rights issues. Women's reproductive rights have become an important component of women's rights.

Notes

1. The International Labor Organization became an agency of the United Nations in 1946 and it was awarded the Nobel Peace Prize on its 50th anniversary. The ILO now has 174 member countries. The Organization works toward it goals to advance a new world economy and to promote political stability throughout the world. The ILO instruments, which are implemented by the International Labor Force Office, deal with the protection of industrial workers from exploitation and improvement of working conditions. They also deal with fundamental rights and freedoms, such as freedom of association, freedom from forced labor, equality of opportunities and treatment in employment, child labor, equality for women, and human rights.

2. As of September 27, 1996, there were 154 countries that had already ratified

CEDAW. The United States is the only developed country in the world that has not passed this treaty. The following is a list of the countries that ratified the treaty. Albania, Algeria, Angola, Antigua & Barbuda, Argentina, Armenia, Australia, Austria, Azerbaijan, The Bahamas, Bangladesh, Barbados, Belarus, Republic, Belgium, Belize, Benin, Bhutan, Bolivia, Bosnia & Herzegovina, Brazil, Bulgaria, Burkina Faso, Burundi, Cambodia, Cameroon, Canada, Cape Verde, Central African Republic, Chad, Chile, China, Colombia, Comoros, Congo, Costa Rica, Cote d'Ivoire, Croatia, Cuba, Cyprus, Czech Republic, Denmark, Dominica, Dominican Republic, Ecuador, Egypt, El Salvador, Equatorial Guinea, Eritrea, Estonia, Ethiopia, Fiji, Finland, France, Gabon, Gambia, Georgia, Germany, Ghana, Greece, Grenada, Guatemala, Guinea, Guinea-Bissau, Guyana, Haiti, Honduras, Hungary, Iceland, India, Indonesia, Iraq, Ireland, Israel, Italy, Jamaica, Japan, Jordan, Kenya, Kuwait, Lao People's Democratic Republic, Latvia, Lesotho, Liberia, Libyan Arab Jamahiriya, Liechtenstein, Lithuania, Luxembourg, Madagascar, Malawi, Malaysia, Maldives, Mali, Malta, Mauritius, Mexico, Mongolia, Morocco, Namibia, Nepal, Netherlands, New Zealand, Nicaragua, Nigeria, Norway, Pakistan, Panama, Papua New Guinea, Paraguay, Peru, Philippines, Poland, Portugal, Republic of Korea, Republic of Macedonia, Republic of Moldavia, Romania, Russian Federation, Rwanda, Saint Kiffs & Nevis, Saint Lucia, Saint Vincent and the Grenadines, Samoa, Senegal, Seychelles, Sierra Leone, Singapore, Slovakia, Slovenia, South Africa, Spain, Sri Lanka, Surinam, Sweden, Tajikistan, Thailand, Togo, Trinidad & Tobago, Tunisia, Turkey, Uganda, Ukranian Republic, United Kingdom of Great Britain & Northern Ireland, United Republic of Tanzania, Uruguay, Uzbekistan, Vanuatu, Venezuela, Viet Nam, Yemen, Yugoslavia, Zaire, Zambia, Zimbabwe. (Source: Ross, Loreffa. September 27, 1996. 'Stop talking and finish women's treaty'. *USA Today.*)

3. Criticisms about the definitions of violence in the draft Declaration is its failure to clarify the standard to be applied in defining state responsibility for violence by nonstate actors. Efforts to eliminate violence against women are identified as measures that states "develop", "consider", "encourage", or "promote" and are thus framed as policy initiatives rather than measures pursuant to human rights standards.

4 Women's Health Movements and Reproductive Rights

The Program of Action of the 1994 International Conference on Population and Development in Cairo defined reproductive health as "a state of complete physical, mental, and social well-being, and not merely the absence of diseases or infirmity, in all matters relating to reproductive system and to its functions and processes" (U.N. Doc. A/CONF. 171/13). The term women's reproductive health is often equated with a satisfying and safe sex life, capacity to reproduce and the freedom to decide if, when, and how to do so. Women's reproductive health is determined by the extent of control over decisions such as marriage, when and with whom to engage in sexual relations, regulation of fertility free from unpleasant or dangerous side effects of contraception, and to have access to information on the prevention and treatment of reproductive illness and unsafe childbirth.

One-half of the world's 2.6 billion women are now in their childbearing years. Illnesses and deaths from complications of pregnancy, childbirth, unsafe abortion, diseases of the reproductive tact, and the improper use of contraceptive methods top the list of health threats to women worldwide (Jacobson, 1991; United Nations, 1995; World Health Organization, 1995).

Of the 150-200 million pregnancies that occur worldwide each year, about 23 million lead to serious complications such as post-partum haemorrhage, hypertensive disorders, eclampsia, puerperal sepsis, and abortion. About half a million of these end with the death of the mother. Ninety-nine percent of these deaths take place in developing countries (United Nations, 1995).

One of the most traumatic family events is the death of the mother. Maternal death has a lasting impact on the emotional and physical well-being of the surviving family members, including children. The economic impact of maternal deaths on the family is high in Sub-Saharan Africa, where more than one third of the women are actively involved in the market economy.

Several research studies in developing countries suggest that about 15 percent of all maternal deaths are due to ectopic pregnancy. One of the immediate causes of ectopic pregnancy is pelvic inflammatory disease, which results in the permanent scarring and narrowing of the fallopian tubes. Women in Africa are about three times more likely to have ectopic pregnancy than women in industrialized countries. The risk of mortality from ectopic pregnancy is very high, especially in rural areas where access to critical care facilities is often lacking.

Traditional practices contribute to maternal mortality in some parts of the world. In Somalia, for example, about 98 percent of the girls undergo female genital mutilation. Globally, about 1.9 million girls undergo genital mutilation each year. Genital mutilation in females is the most important cause of maternal mortality in Somalia. More than 1,600 women per 100,000 live births die of childbirth-related causes. In most industrialized countries fewer than 5 women die per 100,000 live births.

One of the strong incentives for women to have a large number of children in developing countries is high-level infant mortality. Infant mortality in the least developed countries is well above 100 per 1,000 live births. Between 1990 and 1995, infant mortality in developed nations declined from 22 to 12 infant deaths per 1,000 live births. During this period in developing countries, infant mortality dropped from 105 to 69 per 1,000 live births. The regional variations in infant mortality in developing countries are far from being uniform.

The most proximate cause of infant mortality is low birth weight. Approximately one fifth of the children in developing countries are born with low birth weight. Annually more than 12 million children die of malnutrition. Malnourished infants are highly susceptible to contagious diseases. In Nigeria, 200,000 children die every year from diarrhea. In spite of the expanded program in immunization spearheaded by WHO, with the objective of universal immunization by the year 2000, tetanus infection continues to be a major killer. In developing countries, every minute a newborn baby dies of tetanus infection.

The risk of mortality is higher among female infants in countries where male sex preference exists. In China, the one-child-per-couple policy has resulted in a dramatic increase in female infanticide. In developing nations, even if infants survive their first year of life, the risk of death during childhood years continues to be high. One third of the children in Africa are malnourished. Worldwide, about 200 million children were malnourished in the early 1990s.

The capacity to bear children is a basic necessity for the maintenance of reproductive health. The desire for large families is inextricably associated with social and economic factors in developing countries. There is a Yoruba saying, "Children are the clothes of the body. Without children you are naked." Infertility is a major social problem in Sub-Saharan Africa. Infertility is defined as a woman's inability to conceive and bear a child. Infertility among women is more well recognized and adequately investigated than male infertility. There is a well-identified belt of infertility in Africa which extends from the West African nations of Senegal, Upper Ghana, Niger, Mali, northern Nigeria, northwest Cameroon, Gabon, Central African Republic, Zaire, Tanzania, and northwestern regions of Zambia. The reasons for infertility are not well known. Tubal occlusion has been associated with the prevalence of infertility in Kenya (Walton and Mati, 1986). Sexually transmitted diseases (STD) are also associated with primary and secondary infertility.

Sexually transmitted diseases are among the most common diseases in developing countries. The risk of contracting STD is particularly high among adolescents in developing countries. Approximately 5 percent of the youth population is STD infected. One third of all the STD infected are teens in the age group 13-20 years. Teens are a vulnerable population as they are less likely than adults to access health care and seek treatment. Nearly 50 percent of all the HIV infections in developing countries have occurred among young people less than 25 years old. The health care system is under severe stress due to high physician-to-patient ratios. Less than 10 percent of the population in most developing countries depends on secondary and tertiary care facilities where sexually transmitted diseases may be effectively treated.

The incidence of syphilis among women is about 100 times higher in developing countries than in developed nations. The long-term effects of STD have detrimental reproductive health consequences for women. The spread of the diseases of the reproductive tract, such as pelvic inflammatory diseases (PID), may lead to infertility and ectopic pregnancy. The incidence of PID in Africa is very high, with about 360 cases per 100,000 population. If untreated, about 55 to 85 percent of these women with PID may become infertile. In spite of the grave consequences that STDs inflict on their victims, mostly women, the treatment and control of these diseases have been grossly neglected in developing countries.

About one third of the population in the developing world still live in countries where abortion is prohibited or severely restricted to save a woman's life or in case of rape or incest. Thirty-eight million abortions are performed annually in developing countries; 17.6 million are legal, and 20.4 million are illegal. The 1998 International Symposium on Women's Health in the Third World urged governments to eliminate all legal constraints to voluntary abortion and issued a statement deploring the current restrictive policies and pressures dictated by cultural beliefs and political interests (Dixon-Mueller, 1990). Illegal abortion is the leading cause of maternal mortality (Alexander, 1990). An estimate of 100 to 200 thousand women in developing countries die every year from the effects of clandestine abortion (Starrs, 1987; Winikoff and Sullian, 1987). Recent demographic estimates suggest that legalizing abortion and safe abortion services may prevent 20 to 25 percent of the deaths each year from pregnancy-related causes (Dixon-Mueller, 1990). This tide of sorrow and misery among women may be turned by enabling women to take care of themselves. Social and economic institutions currently constrain women from making decisions which benefit them and their children.

In many developing countries, reproductive health objectives are to a great extent defined in terms of increasing contraceptive prevalence and reducing population growth through government-sponsored family planning programs. Women have become program targets to improve contraceptive use and reduce fertility. Family planning programs equated generally with modern contraceptive delivery and fertility reduction are criticized for the lack of measures to ensure women's reproductive health.

Hendriks (1995) identifies the 1980s as the turning point when policy makers, scientists, and women's health and rights activists began to acknowledge the intrinsic relationship between health and human rights. Women's health advocates argue that population control policies and family planning programs should protect personal integrity and provide more holistic approaches to women's health services, particularly in the area of reproductive health (Garcia-Moreno and Claro, 1994) at the expense of current preoccupation with achieving quantitative goals. A 1991 report by the World Health Organization (WHO) and the International Women's Health Coalition suggests that improvements in women's reproductive health inevitably involves empowering women to have control over their own fertility and sexuality under conditions of voluntary choice and minimum health problems. The Cairo Program of Action (1994) recognizes that reproductive rights are human rights which ensure reproductive and sexual health, bodily integrity, and the security of the person.

During the first week of the International Conference on Population and Development (ICPD), contentious issues on abortion and family values emerged. Heated arguments about abortion and family values were sparked by the wording of one paragraph, paragraph 8.25, of the conference draft. Gro Harlem Bruntland, Prime Minister of Norway, was perhaps the most outspoken proponent of women's empowerment and reproductive rights at the conference. She claimed that "morality becomes hypocrisy if it means accepting mothers suffering or dying in connection with unwanted pregnancies and illegal abortions and unwanted children living in misery" (Worzala, 1994). This and a few other changes in wording eventually led the Holy See and its allies to withdraw their objections to the paragraph. The changes read as follows:

> Before: All governments and intergovernmental and non-governmental organizations are urged to deal openly and forthrightly with unsafe abortion as a major public health concern. Governments are urged to assess the health impact of unsafe abortion and to reduce the need for abortion through expanded and improved family planning services. Prevention of unwanted pregnancies must always be given the highest priority and all attempts should be made to eliminate the need for abortion. In no case, should abortion be promoted as a method of family planning. In circumstances where abortion is legal, women who wish to terminate their pregnancies should have ready access to reliable information and compassionate counseling and such abortion should be safe. In all cases, women should have access to services for the management of complications arising from unsafe abortion. Any measures to provide for safe and legal abortion within the health system can only be determined at the national level through policy changes and legislative processes which reflect the diversity of views on the issues of abortion.
>
> After: In no case should abortion be promoted as a method of family planning. All governments and relevant intergovernmental and non-governmental organizations are urged to strengthen their commitment to women's health, to deal with the health impact of unsafe abortion as a major public health concern and to reduce the recourse to abortion through expanded and improved family planning services. Prevention of unwanted pregnancies must always be given the highest priority and all attempts should be made to eliminate the need for abortion. Women who have unwanted pregnancies should have ready access to reliable information and compassionate counseling. Any measures or changes related to abortion within the health system can only be determined at the national or local level according to the national legislative process. In circumstances in which abortion is not against the law, such abortion should be safe. In all cases, women should have access to quality services for the management of complications arising from abortion. Post-abortion counseling, education, and family planning services should be offered promptly which will also help to avoid repeat abortions (Population Network News (PNN), no. 9, Fall 1994).

Three major approaches have emerged which negotiate the relationship between reproductive rights and reproductive health. The demographic approach supports the political goal of controlling population growth through family planning programs while ignoring the rights of individual women to make informed decisions about reproduction and sexuality. Health policies and programs have generally evolved around these family planning and fertility control issues. Overall, world population is still increasing by more than 86 million people annually (World Resources Institute, 1996). Most of the growth occurs in developing countries, especially in Africa, where the population is projected to double between 1995 and 2025. The rapid population growth in many of the developing countries has raised concerns for the well-being of the people. The biomedical approach assumes that a physician's assessment of biological risks is nearly infallible. The near neglect of the social and psychological roots of biological risks results in an over-emphasis on curative medical approaches, which often end up disregarding the right to make voluntary decisions without coercion and pressure. The failure of both the demographic and biomedical approaches lies in their disregard for women's life experiences and denial of the need for gender-sensitive discourse (Whitty, 1996). Throughout the third world, reproductive health risks are excessive because women's low status keeps birth rates high and places health services out of their reach (Jacobson, 1991).

Beginning around 1985, Rosenfield and Maine looked at what is called the maternal child field (MCH Field) and asked the question: "Where is the 'M' in 'MCH'?" In the 1990s, five United Nations conferences were held to address the concept of women's empowerment. The 1994 Cairo Conference focused on the interrelations among population policy, sustainable economic development, and environmental protection. Women's reproductive rights and health were included in each of these discourses.

As Copelon (1995) puts it, the Cairo Program of Action was a watershed in its recognition that reproductive rights are human rights that transcend the "rights to decide freely and responsibly the number and spacing of children" and that include reproductive and sexual health, bodily integrity, and the security of the person, all of which are unattainable without women's empowerment and gender equality.

5 Overview of Rights in Classical and Contemporary Sociological Theories

Emile Durkheim (1893, 1897, 1912) argues that the preservation of norms is essential for achieving integration and solidarity in societies. Durkheimian legal theory focuses on law as a social control factor and an "external" index in the complex moral fabric of social life to help maintain society's collective morality. In *The Division of Labor in Society* (originally published in 1893), Durkheim described the rights of individuals in terms of obligations, sanctions, and morality. In his analysis of the two ideal types of societies, Durkheim (1893/1964) contends that mechanical solidarity is characterized by relatively undifferentiated social structure where there is little or no division of labor. Mechanical solidarity is one of the characteristics of primitive societies. Organic solidarity is obtained in modern societies. As a result of an increase in "dynamic density",[1] modern societies develop a complex division of labor. Organic solidarity is constituted by "collective conscious", a belief shared by the whole community. According to Durkheim, collective conscious is a system of normative constraints that circumscribe individual behavior to the extent that it conforms to the general consensus and/or system of written rules.

In organic societies, the morality and collective conscious that hold society together are rooted in interdependence and formal relations brought about by a highly developed and specialized division of labor. In these societies, individual members are less alike and are more tolerant of dissimilarities. The rights of individual members, according to Durkheim (1893/1964), are essential to reinforce the moral unity and normative boundary lines of society.

The synthetic philosophy of Herbert Spencer on antigovernment individualism asserts that the social whole exists only to facilitate the achievements of its members (Spencer, 1884). The welfare of the members in the society cannot be sacrificed for some supposed benefits of the state, which is to be maintained solely for the benefits of its members. It is the members who possess individual consciousness, and the community as a whole has no corporate consciousness. The corporate life of the society must be subservient to the lives of its members instead of the lives of the members being subservient to the corporate life (Spencer, 1884). In *The Man Versus the State*, Spencer (1884) wrote:

> but it is not so with a society; since its living units do not and cannot lose individual consciousness, and since the community as a whole has no corporate consciousness. This is an everlasting reason why the welfare of citizens cannot rightly be sacrificed to some supposed benefit of the State, and why, on the other hand, the State is to be maintained solely for the benefit of the citizens. The corporate life must be subservient to the lives of the parts, instead of the lives of the parts being subservient to the corporate life. (p.369)

Hence, the functions of governments ought not only guarantee individuals' unmolested pursuit of happiness, but should provide for their happiness (Spencer, 1897).

Spencer (1862) conceives of individual freedom as a societal struggle for survival in which the self-sufficient and the strong will prevail. Society, argues Spencer (1862), is super organic and is organized as a social entity in the same way that a body is organized as a biological entity. Individuals in society, while competing for space, food, and shelter amid scarce resources, move either toward decay or higher states of perfection.

Marx and Engels, unlike Durkheim and Spencer, are highly critical of the principles of rights that emerged from the French Revolution (Sjoberg and Vaughan, 1993). Marx views rights of individuals as class distinct. In *The Communist Manifesto* (published in 1848), Marx and Engels (1848/1972) state that the two polar classes in capitalist societies are based on the ownership of the means of production. Those who own property and the mode of production enjoy personal freedom and rights, which are denied to the workers who do not own property and the mode of production. According to Marx and Engels (1848/1972), the confrontation between the bourgeoisie and the proletariat, the propertied owners and propertyless workers, or those who own the means of production and those who are excluded from such ownership, is inevitable.

Even outside the factory, the proletarian is prey to the bourgeois conspiracy and is exposed to other forms of economic indenture. Alienation and exploitation, Marx declares, are accompanied by desocialization. The proletarian cannot be considered owners of property since they have none. Their families are not families in the bourgeois sense, nor are they citizens of any particular nation in the same way as the bourgeois are citizens. The proletarians have no country. In their lives, law, religion, and morality symbolize nothing but the bourgeois prejudices of society.

Under capitalism, according to Marx, the ownership of the means of production is essential for the enjoyment of rights. The proletarians are deprived of equal rights and suffer from alienation. The separation of the two classes, the bourgeoisie and the proletariat, and the emergence of class consciousness will eventually lead to class conflict resulting in the overthrow of the bourgeoisie. A new classless society will enable the working class to enjoy equal rights. The reproductive rights of working class women are seldom recognized. Women of the working class reproduce to supply the capitalists with a cheap labor force. In a classless society, women's reproductive rights will be recognized, and they will be adequately compensated for their reproductive labor.

Max Weber (1921/1968), however, believed that individuals in modern societies are incapable of resisting the iron cage of bureaucratic life. The "steel-hard cage" of modern and bureaucratic instrumentalism is, in large part, escape-proof. Nobody can evade the possibility of being a cog in a bureaucratic machine and cheerful robots (Mills, 1961).

> Rational calculation . . . reduces every worker to a cog in this bureaucratic machine and seeing himself in this light, he will merely ask how to transform himself into somewhat a bigger cog. . . . The passion of bureaucratization drives us to despair. (Weber, 1921/1968, p.Iiii)

Weber (1921/1968) defined bureaucracy as one of the structural forms of legal authority. The Weberian tradition addresses the contribution to the formation of economic and political structure (Conterrell, 1991).

Modern society, according to Weber (1921/1968), is a form of bureaucracy that is characterized by a complex division of labor, a conception of rationality, and a hierarchy of authority and power. One of the most important sociological questions for Weber is the issue of how power confines the individual's "free choices" in social life. Weber (1962) defined power as the probability that one actor within a social relationship will be in a position to carry out his or her own will despite resistance. According to Weber (1962), the state secures its privileged position by establishing a "monopoly of the legitimate use of physical force in the enforcement of its order" (p.154). Weber (1962) maintains that states posses any of the three types of authority-traditional, charismatic, and rational-legal. The choice is only between bureaucracy and dilettantism in the field of administration (Weber, 1962).

"Mean-ends rationality" and "value rationality" are mechanisms for achieving personal goals in modern societies (Weber, 1962, p.223). Freedom in modern societies is a result of activities and decisions arising from informed choices. The modern society provides individuals with leisure and material comfort as a result of scientific and technological development. The trend toward a high degree of rationalization is constraining and at times inhumane. Human values and freedoms are compromised to achieve efficiency, calculability, and predictability. The role of large-scale organizations in modern societies is undermining human rights.

Parsons (1951), like Weber, believed that human action adapts to the needs of society through four functional imperatives: adaptation (A), goal attainment (G), integration (I), and latency (or pattern maintenance) (L). The AGIL action scheme functions at all levels of the social system, the cultural system, the personality system, and the behavioral organism. Parsons (1951) defined social systems in terms of their normative structure. He viewed the basic unit of the social system as the "status-role". Status refers to a structural position within the social system, and role is what the actor does in such a position. The social system enables the socialization of its actors, whose need-dispositions may be satisfied under the constraints of social control and individual conformity. Individuals perform their AGIL action in the social system by means of their adaptation to the subsystems of economy, polity, the fiduciary system, and the societal community.

Parsons (1951) defined cultural system as an ordered system of symbols which become objects of orientation to actors and constitute internalized aspects of the personality system. Because of its symbolic and subjective characteristic, the cultural system, according to Parsons (1951), is the major force binding the action system. The transmission of one social system to another takes place through diffusion, and the transmission of one personality system to another takes place through learning and socialization.

The personality system, according to Parsons (1951), is the organized system of orientation. The motivation for action derives socialization under given social and cultural systems. The system becomes "an independent system through its relations to its own life experience" (Parsons, 1970, p.82). The basic component of the personality is the "need-disposition".[2]

Parsons (1951) identified three types of need-dispositions. The first type impels actors to seek love and approval from social relationships; the second type includes internalized values that lead actors to conform to cultural standards; and the third type is role expectations that lead actors to give and get appropriate responses. The fourth component of Parson's action system is the behavioral organism.[3] It is the source of energy for the other three systems and is based on genetic constitution.

Parsons' structural functionalism, based on the AGIL scheme involving the four actions systems, therefore presents a picture of "the freedom of human action" that is circumscribed by the social structure and internalized by human adaptive skills. Sjoberg and Vaughan (1993), based on Weber's bureaucratic structure theory and Parsons' AGIL action schemes, identified four systems of bureaucratic structure within the global context that maintain the freedom of choice of individuals in society.

The first system consists of organizations associated with finance capital that shape the economic and political and even the cultural orientations of nation-states. The second system is the large-scale bureaucratic structures that have emerged in the form of the technological/scientific/educational complex, whose significance stems from the fact that modern economic systems depend on scientific innovation. The third set of organizations refers to the mass media, which serve to shape the nature of public opinions.

The final bureaucratic complex is related to the production of goods. Individuals, Sjoberg and Vaughan (1993) argue, are influenced by these bureaucratic organizations. These bureaucratic structures mold the manner in which individuals interact with one another, and they limit the alternatives. The rights of people under modern economies are thus affected by the bureaucratic structures.

Both classical and contemporary sociological theories have broadly touched on the issue of rights. These theories hardly address women's reproductive rights in particular. Sociological studies that have attempted to formulate conceptual model of reproductive rights are few.

Notes

1. Durkheim (1893/1964) defined "dynamic density" as the increase in population size and interaction among people.

2. Parsons (1951) differentiated need-dispositions from drives, the former being the most significant units of motivation of action, the latter being the physiological energy that makes action possible. In other words, need-dispositions are drivers that are shaped by the social setting and acquired through the process of action itself; whereas the innate drive is part of the biological organism.

3. Parsons (1970), in his later works, labeled "behavioral organism" as "behavioral system" (p.104).

6 Explanations of Reproductive Rights

It was indicated that reproductive rights in developing countries have three broad sources. The first source is the population control movement with its sometimes coercive tendencies and the undesirable health outcomes of modern contraceptive technology among women in developing countries. Very often, coercive methods of birth control are combined with the exploitation of women for contraceptive research. The political backlash spearheaded by women's organizations against the violation of women's bodies provided sustenance to the reproductive rights movement. Secondly, in recent times, the growth of women's health programs has emphasized the importance of reproductive rights as a precondition for improvements in women's health globally. A third source is the long-term evolution of human rights values during the last three centuries. Changes in values and political reactions against overzealous birth control delivery systems bring about changes in the social institutions related to reproduction. These three broad sources are associated with social structural factors. The levels of reproductive rights in developing countries may be accounted for by social structural factors.

Current sociological research on reproductive rights has several drawbacks. First, sociologists have not adequately developed theoretical models of rights (Turner, 1993). Classical works of Durkheim (1893, 1895, 1897, 1912), Weber (1921), and Veblen (1914, 1921) clearly pointed to the role of rights in modern societies. They argue that preservation of rights is essential for achieving integrity and solidarity in society and allude to a structural basis for the emergence of norms. Weber (1921) suggests that economic development, more specifically capitalistic development is a factor in the development of legal norms. Unlike Marx, Weber sees economy as the primary force influencing law. He placed the effects of economy on law alongside those of political and social factors and policies. However, these theoretical insinuations have not been adequately utilized for formulating sociological models of reproductive rights.

Secondly, current studies on human rights are limited to the political and legal aspects of human rights (Cook, 1992, 1993, 1995; Correa and Petchesky,

1994; Isaacs, 1995; Sjoberg et al., 1995). Very few attempts have been made at empirically testing the relationship between socioeconomic factors and reproductive rights cross-nationally.

Current studies of reproductive rights (McDaniel, 1985; Petchesky, 1990; Dixon-Mueller, 1993; Li, 1993; Fathella, 1994; Germain et al., 1994; Isaacs, 1995), ignore the need to assess the empirical relationship between reproductive rights and structural changes due to socioeconomic development. Finally, most feminist empirical analyses "have been case studies and have not engaged the conceptual frameworks and empirical finding of the mainstream literature" (Orloff, 1993, p. 304).

In this chapter, we attempt to propose explanations for the current levels of reproductive rights in developing countries. Resources such as education, improvement in women's status, and relief from domestic duties by having small families are essential components of a resource base for the realization of reproductive rights demands.

The empowerment model advocates reinforcing women's power by investing in a variety of attributes such as human capital and small family size (Hartman, 1987). More importantly, as women gain fertility control, resulting in fertility decline, they will have the time and energy resources to demand and acquire reproductive rights. Thus, fertility decline may provide a necessary condition for women to gain reproductive rights. We argue that small family size and slow population growth rates are important determinants of reproductive rights in developing countries. Fertility decline may be brought about by factors such as family planning, women's education, gender equality, and economic development. These factors may influence reproductive rights levels through fertility.

We introduce a model in which fertility level is the most proximate determinant of changes in reproductive rights levels in developing countries. The theoretical model involves three major explanations, namely, the population growth explanation, the women's education explanation, and the gender equality explanation. As indicated in chapter 3, opinions and agreements favorable to and supportive of reproductive rights partly result from international conventions and conferences such as the 1968 International Conference on Human Rights held in Tehran. The impact of these global agreements on national laws is painfully slow. As a result, the effect of value factors on reproductive rights level is not likely to be realized in the short run. In sharp contrast, the effort of state-supported policies on reproductive rights is likely to be immediate. The sociological model we propose focuses on the structural factors which influence reproductive rights cross-nationally.

Population Growth Explanation

It was not until the late 1980s that the relationship between fertility decline and women's reproductive rights became a hotly debated topic both in academia and in international conventions. The relationship is, however, left underexplored empirically. How does limiting the number of children influence the exercise of women's reproductive rights?

First, limiting or avoiding births enables women to exercise more freedom within marriages or consensual unions. Women who delay or avoid births experience significant economic advantages over those with large families. Having small families can improve a woman's ability to end an unsatisfactory relationship with few personal costs (Dixon-Mueller, 1993). Having a large family, on the contrary, intensifies women's vulnerability and limits their capacity to exercise equal rights with men during marriage or at its dissolution. Second, limiting or avoiding births enables women to exercise their political rights fully. Ware (1993) argues that one of the major factors that restricts women from gaining autonomy and personal rights for reproductive decision is childcare responsibilities. Declining fertility is likely to free women from childbearing and rearing burdens and increase the possibility of participation in civil and political organizations outside the household. Motherhood may constrain women from freedom of movement and opportunities for social activities, and it may further reduce personal autonomy (Sogner, 1993). Having large families may inhibit women's acquisition of earning assets (Heitlinger, 1993) and intensify women's vulnerability and likelihood of dependence on men for economic and social support.

The inability to gain reproductive rights is perhaps associated with the "culture of silence", the powerlessness of women as a group in society. Historian Rosalind Petchesky (1990) states that the right to choose means little when women are powerless as a group in the society. Limiting or avoiding births may provide more time and energy and increase the opportunities for women to participate in education, paid employment, and community work. Small family size enables women to assert their demands for resources and technologies which may enhance their autonomy and improve their reproductive rights and well-being. Extrafamilial involvement will enable women to organize themselves as a social group to break through the "culture of silence". The rise in women's power may increase the level of reproductive rights. Thus, population growth is likely to have negative impact on women's reproductive rights. The slower the population growth rate, the more the women's reproductive rights.

One of the major components of fertility decline is the "modern contraceptive revolution" fueled by government-sponsored family planning programs worldwide (Lapham and Mauldin, 1985). These programs in developing countries provide birth control knowledge, increase the use of contraceptive devices, and improve the availability of and accessibility to birth control services and technologies. Family planning programs lower market costs by providing information about birth control services free or below costs, and also lower subjective costs by lending legitimacy to practicing family planning and birth control (Easterlin, 1975).

Population control policies in developing countries have come to be equated with fertility reduction policies. These programs have mobilized huge material resources and expert support mechanisms (Jain and Bruce, 1993; Zurayk et al., 1994). Global data on family planning policies (Ross et al., 1993) suggest that family planning has now become a state-led policy worldwide and has had a negative impact on fertility. Global contraceptive sales climbed to 2.6 billion U.S. dollars per year during the 1990s (Fathalla, 1994). Substantial fertility declines have been recorded in developing countries. Nearly all have occurred during a period when family planning facilities have been made widely available (Caldwell, 1982). Lapham and Mauldin (1985) suggest that family planning program effort in developing countries can reduce fertility in the absence of social and economic development. Family planning program effort is likely to reduce population growth. The greater the family planning program effort, the slower the population growth.

A second factor that affects population growth is social and economic development brought about by modernization, which is perhaps one of the most important agents of transformation of social structures at a global level in the 20th century. Although modernization processes follow different patterns in different countries, the characteristics of the modernization processes are common to all (Kerr et al., 1994). Modernization refers to the process of economic and social changes brought about by the introduction of an industrial mode of production. Robertson (1981) defines modernization as a process that accompanies technologically induced economic growth. The process is sweeping the globe as the less developed nations of the world follow the patterns established by the more advanced industrial societies (Robertson, 1981). Modernization affects virtually every aspect of society, including physical, social, and economic infrastructures involved in the production, distribution, and consumption of services.

Boserup (1970) maintains that a reduction in the proportion of the population engaged in agriculture goes hand-in-hand with economic development. The percentage of labor force in agriculture decreases, and the proportion of people engaged in industry and services increases. The changes in sustenance organization necessitate frequent changes in skills, responsibilities, and occupational composition (Kerr et al., 1994). Moore (1965) contends that the first-order consequences of industrialization involve a labor force shift from one economic sector to another (from agriculture and fishing to industry and service), and an increase in women's status.

The development and increasing role of science and technology as a result of the processes of modernization produce four types of consequences which may affect people's motivation to have children. First, industrialization brings about a shift in the patterns of employment. The percentage of labor force in agriculture decreases, and the proportion of people engaged in industry and services increases. As a result of the shift from agriculture to industry and the demand for labor force in industry, migration from rural areas to urban industrial bases increases.

An increase in the urbanization rate provides people with several alternatives for employment and opportunities for social mobility, which, in turn, may hasten socioeconomic development and urbanization. Easterlin and Crimmins (1985) state that urbanization and the shift from agriculture to industry or service reduce the demand for children by lowering the price of goods relative to children and increasing alternative life chances.

Secondly, the transition from a subsistence economy to a semi-modern or modern-town economy results in a highly specialized and complex division of labor. The social relations created by a complex system of division of labor may imply new hierarchical relations in the work place and opportunities for upward social mobility. Expectations and opportunities for social mobility may increase. Having children per se rarely satisfies as an end in itself but is generally a means to other ends (Coale, 1973). The perceived advantages of having fewer children may lead to fertility decline.[1]

Thirdly, the change in social relationships due to urbanization and the increasing proportion of labor force in industry and service sectors may have an effect on ideological changes and changes in lifestyle and family structure. The emergence of conjugal and nuclear families and demands for leisure time may reduce the motivation for having large families.

Finally, the development of science and technology due to modernization processes, together with changes in the social structure, may lead to modifications in belief systems and further may enhance women's status and autonomy for making decisions to have small families.

The classical demographic transition theories link the process of industrialization to fertility. Warren Thompson (1929) categorized countries into three main groups according to their patterns of population growth in relation to socioeconomic development. Group A (GA): countries (e.g., the United States, Northern and Western Europe) that have moved from high rates of natural increases to low rates of natural increases. Group B (GB): countries (e.g., Central Europe) with a decline in both death and birth rates, but probably a more rapid decline in death rates. Group C (GC): the rest of the world, with little evidence of control over either births or deaths. Sixteen years after Thompson's work, Frank Notestein (1945) provided labels for the three types of growth patterns: GA pattern as "incipient decline", GB pattern as "transitional growth", and GC pattern as "high growth potentia". Demographic transition proceeds in three sequential stages (Notestein,1945). In the first stage, there is high growth potential because both birth and death rates are high. This usually happens in countries with lower levels of social and economic development. The second-stage transition is from high to low birth and death rates. The growth potential is realized as death rate drops precede birth rate drops. In the final stage, both death and birth rates drop. This pattern of population change is found in countries with high levels of development (Weinstein, 1976).

Huber's (1973) historical overview of societies from preindustrial to industrial describes how technological changes lead to fertility decline.

> Industrialization first turned the cost-benefit ratio of children upside down. Then wives were drawn into the labor force, raising the opportunities cost of their time and thereby the cost of children. Now below-replacement fertility in the West has highlighted the problem of population maintenance. Parenthood may have to be made more attractive by limiting the hours of responsibility. But [this] would raise women's status in the family and in society in ways that were unimaginable a few decades ago. (Chapter 1)

Social and economic development is likely to have a negative effect on population growth. The higher the levels of socioeconomic development, the slower the population growth.

A third factor that affects population growth is women's education. One of the direct consequences of the increase in women's education is the decline in fertility. Women's education is positively related to contraceptive knowledge and use and negatively related to family size in high-fertility countries (Dixon-Mueller, 1993). Most studies show that the educational level of the wife is more strongly and inversely correlated with family size than is the educational level of the husband after controlling for other influences (Cleland and Rodriguez, 1988). Nearly everywhere in the world, educated women have fewer children than women who are not educated (Weeks, 1994). Educated women are less likely to marry and to bear large number of children. In spite of variations in methodology and the sources of data over the past 30 years, this view of women is consistent (Coale, 1973; Watkins, 1993).

Data suggested that one of the more common characteristics of those areas was the rapid spread of women's education. Dixon-Mueller (1993) states that education beyond the primary level is often associated with factors such as an openness to new ideas, a higher standard of living, exposure to an urban environment, higher occupational achievement, and a greater range of other options and interests outside the home. Any of these may be responsible for the apparent influence of education on fertility.

Women's education affects fertility in three ways: first, by delaying marriage and increasing the probability of non-marriage; second, by creating aspirations for higher standards of living and by stimulating their interest and involvement in activities outside home. Strong labor force participation promotes concerns about child quality (Becker, 1960) and fosters individualistic values (Lesthaeghe and Surkyn, 1988) and consumer aspirations (Easterlin, 1975, 1978). These factors tend to reduce fertility independent of relative cohort size. Finally, women's education increases the exposure to contraceptive knowledge, creates favorable attitudes toward birth control, and increases contraceptive use (Dixon-Mueller, 1993).

Women's education is likely to reduce population growth. The higher the educational levels of women, the lower the rate of population growth.

The rate of population growth is associated with gender equality. "The gender structure determinants of fertility were until recently 'a black box' to demography" (McDaniel, 1996, p.85). McDaniel (1996) calls for greater attention to "women as agents, players, and pawns in power systems and struggles" to explain fertility patterns (p.86). In general, gender equality has a negative relationship with fertility. Gender equality has direct impact on women's ability to determine the number and spacing of their children.

One obstacle to gender equality is the strong influence of patriarchal systems. According to Dixon-Mueller (1993), in patriarchal societies women have little control over the timing and number of children they expect to bear.

> Patriarchy has both a material base and an ideological justification. The material base involves, to varying degrees, control by elder male heads of a linkage, extended family, and/or household, or by the male in a couple, over the means of production and reproduction, that is, over valued property and its uses; over family (especially female) labor and its returns; and over the circumstances under which family (especially female) members enter and leave sexual unions and have children. The ideological justification consists of assertions in various forms of the 'natural' or 'divine' origins of filial obligation, male dominance, and female subordination, their expression in legal and moral codes of behavior. (p.24)

The patriarchal system perpetuates gender-based division of labor. Male control over women affects fertility in the following ways. First, the patriarchal system values women for bearing and rearing children. As a result, a significant portion of the cost of children is shifted to women. Husbands may benefit from children's labor, but bear few of the costs of their rearing. Hence, they have little incentive to reduce fertility (Kritz and Gurak, 1989). Secondly, in patriarchal societies male descendents, in particular, are highly valued. Patriarchal communities deprive women of their right to make reproductive decisions while extolling the spiritual and economic gains of having children. This contributes to the positive value of children and increases the demand for large family size. Finally, patriarchal families impose the will of both the older family members and the males on the women in the family. The reproductive behavior of women is controlled by the older members and the males in the family, who impose family-level fertility expectations on women. Male dominance tends to facilitate high rates of fertility (Keyfitz, 1986). On the contrary, an egalitarian relationship between men and women in the society leads to gender equality in family relationships. Egalitarian relationships enable women to make independent decisions with regard to starting, spacing, and stopping family formation. Gender equality is likely to reduce population growth. The higher the levels of gender equality, the lower the population growth.

Women's Education Explanation

Women's education perspective argues that an increase in women's educational level is likely to enhance their ability and power in reproductive decision making. Education serves as one of the most important means of obtaining knowledge. The appearance of individual values and the search for personal autonomy are often followed by an increase in education. Ideas of rights that call for democratization and respect for individual freedom stem in large part from education. Women with more education are more likely to be aware of their rights. The attainment of the same level of education with men is a precondition to women's autonomy (Julemont, 1993). The ideology of reproductive rights is brought about by women for women through education (Correa, 1994). As a result, a higher level of women's education is likely to lead to a higher level of reproductive rights.

An increase in the human capital increases the likelihood of women achieving equal status with their male counterparts. Education as a human resource may provide women with ideas that challenge and question traditional values and heighten the motivation to demand equality. The education of women may also enhance women's ability to selectively utilize a wide range of ideas and values for personal advancement. Education tends to increase the opportunities for women to participate in the process of modernization and organize as a social group for bringing about changes in economic and social institutions (Correa, 1994).

Education provides skills and opportunities for out-of-home employment. Social and economic benefits are more likely to accrue when women are ensured of sufficient education and employment that provide income over which they have direct control. This, in turn, offers women basic economic security and improvement in their social status. A positive change in the aggregate level of human capital among women is likely, to an extent, to reduce the gap between men and women in terms of their status in society.

Education enables women to make use of opportunities in the labor market, which is likely to broaden their horizons, introduce new forms of authority, and threaten power relations within the family. Schooling is likely to enable women to widen their social networks, gain new reference groups, and prepare women to take advantage of opportunities in public spheres. Women's education is likely to increase their reproductive rights and increase the level of gender equality. The higher the levels of women's education, the higher the levels of gender equality.

One of the most important effects of socioeconomic development on women's life chances is the increase in women's educational attainment. Economic development processes demand the upgrading of skills, and therefore schooling becomes a prerequisite for both males and females in entering the modern world. Public education becomes more accessible and affordable as a result of industrialization, especially in urban areas. The accessibility and affordability of public education and the rising expectations among women tend to increase the proportion of women who enter school and pursue their education. The higher the levels of socioeconomic development, the higher the levels of women's education.

The second factor that contributes to women's education is secularization. Hess, Markson, and Stein (1996) state that one crucial dimension of modernization is the process of secularization, a process that focuses on the ability of human reason and technology to solve problems. The secularization thesis points to at least two dimensions. The first dimension is the transformation from communities to societies,[2] and the second is rationalization.[3] Kelly and Cutright (1980) associated secularization with industrialization and modernization.

The 11th Congress of the International Humanist and Ethical Union, held at the Free University of Brussels in Belgium in August 1990, suggested that liberty, equality, and fraternity are all components of secularization. A secular society is therefore a democratic society characterized by its political and civil freedoms. The political and civil freedoms due to secularization processes make it possible to increase the status of women and their participation in educational and economic activities.

The transition from community to society and the process of rationalization brought about by the secularization of society enhance women's educational attainment. Secularization is likely to increase women's education. The higher the levels of secularization, the higher the levels of women's education.

Gender Equality Explanation

A third perspective focuses on the role of gender in the development of reproductive rights. The extent of gender equality has direct impact on women's ability to determine the number and spacing of their children and on the control over their reproductive behavior. Gender relationships are embedded in social, economic, and political institutions and are reinforced through everyday interactions. All social, economic, and political institutions have rules and norms to facilitate gender relations. Women's reproductive choice is influenced by the distribution of resources in the community and opportunity structures resulting from the interaction between men and women. When the unequal distribution of social resources between the two sexes favors males, patriarchy allocates intrafamilial power in favor of males. Mason and Palan (1981) defined the patriarchal system as a set of social institutions that limit women's opportunities to be self-supporting, thereby making them dependent on male relatives for survival. Patriarchal control has direct impact on women's reproductive decision-making.

The system of domination subordinates women through public patriarchy (in public spheres of economies and states) and private patriarchy (in the family). The system of domination creates structural obstacles for women to acquire social resources necessary to make reproductive decisions. Orloff (1993) argues that current state social provisions undermine women's abilities to gain reproductive rights. In patriarchal societies women have little control over the circumstances under which they live, the returns of their labor, their sexuality, and the timing and number of children (Dixon-Mueller, 1993). Gender inequalities constrain women's opportunities for employment in comparison to men's. The disparity in employment between men and women reduces the economic independence of women. The resource theory holds that, the greater the material and social resources a woman brings into her marriage relative to those of her husband, the greater is her ability to make reproductive decisions. Women as a group have fewer social and economic resources than men. As a result, women are constrained in their abilities to make and implement reproductive decisions. Gender equality is likely to increase women's reproductive rights. The higher the levels of gender equality, the more the reproductive rights for women.

The extent of gender equality is affected by social and economic development. Socioeconomic development affects gender equality in the following ways: first, technological revolution fueled by industrialization plays a crucial role in economic development. Economic growth is by and large associated with the rising demand for labor and socioeconomic opportunities. This process is made possible by the rapid growth of industrial investment in the city, fueling a demand for labor. As a result, a large number of women are likely to become wage earners. Women's labor force participation increases their economic independence and challenges the traditional image of women as merely child bearers and child rearers. The changes in women's status and roles bring to the forefront new issues with regard to gender equality. Blumberg (1991) argues that control over economic resources is the main (though not the sole) correlate of gender equality.

Modernization theories suggest that social and economic development provides women access to key resources, such as education and paid employment, and alters traditional family systems. Social and economic development provides women with increasing opportunities for education and vocational training. As women's human capital and economic status increase, there is likely to be a decline in gender inequality. These consequences of modernization free women from many constraints. Modernization tends to have a positive effect on gender equality. Socioeconomic development is likely to increase gender equality. The higher the levels of socioeconomic development, the greater the gender equality.

Secularization has an effect on gender equality. The secularization thesis argues that there is a diminution in the social significance of religion and a growth in the reliance on technology and rational calculation. With the diminishing authority of religious institutions and a widespread quest for rational knowledge, the mythical and artistic interpretations of nature and society tend to be displaced by scientific and logical thinking. In this new "age of reason", the traditional norms that guide people's actions are challenged by practical and egalitarian beliefs and practices. The processes of secularization may entail a shift from religious to secular control over people's everyday activities. The shift in beliefs and practices will result in redefinition of the roles and status of women. Secularization is likely to increase gender equality. The higher the levels of secularization, the greater the gender equality.

The proposed model of reproductive rights attempts to integrate the three explanations of women's reproductive rights and specifies the effects of family planning programs and modernization processes on women's reproductive rights in developing nations. Figure 6.1 presents the hypothesized model.

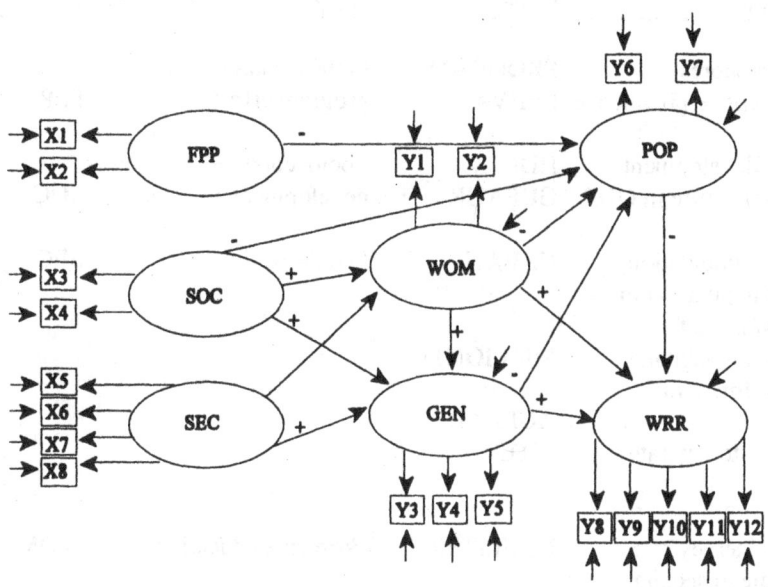

Figure 6.1   The proposed model of women's reproductive rights

Note: See Table 6.1 for variable definitions. Exogenous factors are interrelated.

Table 6.1 **Variable names and definitions**

Variable definition	Variable name	Latent variable definition	Latent variable name
Program scores	PROGRAM	Family planning	
Contraceptive prevalence	PREVA	program effort	FPP
Human development	HDI	Socioeconomic	
% of agriculture in GDP	GDPAGR	development	SOC
% Urban population	URBAN	Secularization	SEC
% total population in cities w/at least 1 million inhabitants	MILLION1		
% labor force in agriculture	AGRLAB		
% adult literacy rate	LITER		
Female literacy rate	FEMLITER	Women's education	WOM
% female in secondary schools	FEMSEC		
Female-male ratio of mean years of schooling	FMMEAN	Gender equality	GEN
Political-legal equality for women	POLEQUAL		
Socioeconomic equality for women	SOEQUAL		
Total fertility rate	FERTI	Population growth	POP
Average annual growth rate	GROWTH		
Legal abortion right	ABORTION	Women's reproductive rights	WRR
Personal rights to interracial, interreligious or civil marriages	INTERRAC		

Table 6.1   Variable names and definitions (cont'd.)

Personal rights for equality of sexes during marriage and for divorce proceedings	DIVORCE
Personal rights to use contraceptive pills and devices	PILLS
Support of distribution of contraceptive devices	SUPPORT

Notes

1. Ansley Coale (1973), in his revised approach to demographic transition, states that there are three preconditions for a substantial fertility decline: (1) the acceptance of calculated choice as a valid element in marital fertility; (2) the perception of advantages from reduced fertility; and (3) knowledge and mastery of effective techniques of control.

2. In his *Community and Society* (1887/1963), German sociologist Ferdinand Tonnies refers to the social evolution from traditional society to modern (rational) society as *Gemeinschaft* and *Gesellschaft*.

Gemeinschaft consists of social relationships of an intimate or primary characteristic. Within the Gemeinschaft form of social order, a homogeneity of views, the ties of kinship, a common language, and a sense of place are the basis of mechanical unity (solidarity). Social control is left to consensus, custom, religious precept, and physical punishment for deviance.

Gesellschaft represents the society in which there exists impersonal mean-to-end forms of social relationships. The identity of the community surrenders to the anonymity of mass society. Social relationships are based on special needs, class interests, and heterogeneity, a characteristic of organic solidarity.

3. Max Weber (1921/1968) defined rationality on the basis of action. Weber differentiated between two types of rationality, mean-to-ends and value rationality (Ritzer, 1996). Kalberg (1980) identified four basic types of rationality in Weber's work. They are practical rationality, theoretical rationality, substantive rationality, and formal rationality.

7 Methodology

The focus on the legal aspects of human rights nationally and cross-nationally has in general led to a lack of emphasis on the social-structural basis of rights. As a result, data on cross-national reproductive rights are seldom limited with cross-national socioeconomic data. The emphasis on socioeconomic factors influencing reproductive rights in this study necessitates the creation of a data set containing socioeconomic variables and measures of reproductive rights.

This chapter is divided into two sections. The first section of this chapter describes the sources of data. The second section focuses on analytical strategies. The proposed model is composed of several latent factors such as secularization. In addition, the suggested model of reproductive rights specifies the theoretical linkages among the latent factors. The test of the model involves the estimation of the strength and direction of the proposed causal paths.

The model estimation is done in several stages. First, all the proposed indicators of the latent factors are described. Aggregate measures such as mean and median are used to describe the indicators. Another important source of variation of the indicators is region. The spatial properties of the variables are described by examining the aggregate measures of indicators for selected regions of the developing countries. In the second stage of analysis, the reliability and validity of the scales used to measure the latent factors are assessed. Confirmatory factor analysis is used to assess the reliability and validity of the latent factors. The final stage of analysis employs structural equation modeling. This method is appropriate for testing causal models with latent factors.

The Sources of Data and Measurement of the Variables

The cross-national analysis involves 101 developing countries as identified by the World Bank. Thirty-nine are in Sub-Saharan Africa; 24, in Latin America/Caribbean; 16, in Middle East/North Africa; and 23, in Asia. Due to lack of data, Taiwan has been dropped from the study. Data for the study are obtained from a number of sources. Table 7.1 presents the sources of data. The exogenous factors in this study are family planning program effort (FPP), socioeconomic development (SOC), and secularization (SEC).

Lapham and Mauldin (1985) conceptualized family planning program effort as "the sum of policies adopted and implemented; the activities carried out to provide family planning knowledge, supplies, and services; the availability and accessibility of fertility regulation methods; and the monitoring and evaluation of all of these" (p.120). The four components of program effort are "policies, resources, and stage-setting activities"; "service and service-related activities"; "statistical record-keeping, evaluation, and management's use of evaluation findings"; and "availability and accessibility: contraception, sterilization, and abortion" (Lapham and Mauldin, 1985, p.120).

Table 7.1   Data sources for the variables

Variables	Sources
Family planning program effort scores	Ross, A.J., W.P. Mauldin, and V.C. Miller. (1993). *Family Planning and Population: A Compendium of International Statistics*
Contraceptive prevalence	Ross, A.J., W.P. Mauldin, and V.C. Miller. (1993). *Family Planning and Population: A Compendium of International Statistics*
Human development index	United Nations Development Program. (1992). *Human Development Report*.
% agriculture in GDP	World Resources Institute. (1992). *World Resources 1992-93*. World Bank. (1994). *Social Indicators of Development*.
Urban population as a % of the total	World Resources Institute. (1992). *World Resources 1992-1993*. World Bank. (1993). *World Tables*.
% population in cities w/at least 1 million inhabitants	World Resources Institute. (1992). *World Resources 1992-93*.
% labor force in agriculture	World Bank. (1994). *Social Indicators of Development*.
Adult literacy rate	World Resources Institute. (1992). *World Resources 1992-93*.

Table 7.1   Data sources for the variables (cont'd.)

Adult female literacy rate	World Resources Institute. (1992). *World Resources 1992-1993.*
% female of relevant age enrolled in secondary schools	World Bank. (1994b). *World Development Report.* World Bank. (1994a). *Social Indicators of Development.*
Female-male ratio of mean years of schooling	World Resources Institute. (1992). *World Resources 1992-1993.*
Political-legal equality for women	Humana, Charles. (1992). *World Human Rights Guide.*
Social-economic equality for women	Humana, Charles. (1992). *World Human Rights Guide*
Total fertility rate	World Resources Institute. (1992). *World Resources 1992-93.*
Average annual growth rate	World Resources Institute. (1992). *World Resources 1992-93.*
Legal abortion right	Ross, A.J.. W.P. Mauldin, and V.C. Miller. (1993). *Family Planning and Population: A Compendium of International Statistics.* Dixon-Mueller, Ruth. (1993). *Population Policy and Women's Rights.*
Personal rights to interracial, interreligious or civil marriages	Humana, Charles. (1992). *World Human Rights Guide.*
Personal rights for equality of sexes during marriages and for divorce proceedings	Humana, Charles. (1992). *World Human Rights Guide.*
Personal rights to use contraceptive devices	Humana, Charles. (1992). *World Human Rights Guide.*
Support for distribution of contraceptives	United Nations. (1995). *Global Population Policy Data Base.*

Family planning program effort is measured by family planning program effort scores (PROGRAM) and prevalence of contraceptive use (PREVA).[1] Family planning program effort scores are obtained from Lapham and Mauldin's 30-item program effort scores (1989). The variable ranges from 0 to 120.[2] Contraceptive prevalence data for 1990 are for all countries, based on available information (Ross et al., 1993). Contraceptive prevalence is defined as the percentage of couples in the reproductive ages (15-44) using contraception at a given time (Mauldin and Segal, 1988). Estimates are based on the number of first-time acceptors of a family planning method, multiplied by a dropout or a discontinuation factor. Contraceptive prevalence is measured by a ratio scale that ranges from 0 to 100 percent.

"Previous concept of development has often given exclusive attention to economic growth, on the assumption that growth will ultimately benefit everyone" (United Nations Development Program, 1992, p.13). The United Nations Development Program (1992) proposed a new measure, the Human Development Index (HDI), for the measurement of socioeconomic development. The first report by the United Nations Development Program in 1992 defined human development as "a process of enlarging people's choices" (United Nations Development Program, 1992, p.12). Income is certainly one of those choices, but it is by no means the only one.[3] Socioeconomic development refers to both the human and the economic development of a country. The HDI ranges from 0 to 1 and is used to indicate levels of human development.[4]

A second indicator of socioeconomic development is agriculture as a percentage of the distribution of gross domestic product (GDPAGR). It refers to the percentage of gross domestic product spent on agriculture. The variable is measured by a ratio scale that ranges from 0 to 100 percent.

Secularization is defined as the extent to which one feels a sense of responsibility for one's own well-being, or personal autonomy. Leasure (1989) defined secularization as an attitude (or spirit) of autonomy from otherworldly powers and a sense of responsibility for one's own well-being. Theories of secularization suggest several indicators. They are urban population as a percentage of total population (URBAN), percentage of total population in cities with at least 1 million inhabitants (MILLION1), thousands percent of labor force in agriculture (AGRLAB), and percentage of adult literacy (LITER).[5]

Urban population as a percentage of total population and the percentage of total population in cities with 1 million or more inhabitants are based on midyear population estimates. These indicators are measured by ratio scales. Percentage of total population in cities with at least 1 million inhabitants is calculated using figures for populations of urban agglomerations of 1 million or more residents.[6]

The intervening dimensions are women's education (WOM), gender equality (GEN), and population growth (POP). Women's education refers to personal knowledge resulting from schooling among women. The observed variables for the construct are percentage of adult female literacy (FEMLIT) and percentage of females of relevant age enrolled in secondary schools (FEMSEC). Percentage of adult female literacy is estimated as the percentage of people over age 15 who can read and write in the total population. The data sources for the variable, percentage of females of relevant ages enrolled in secondary schools (1990), are from the *World Development Report* and *Social Indicators* by the World Bank. The two indicators for women's education are measured by using a ratio scale of 0 to 100 percent.

Gender inequality refers to the parity between men and women in their life chances. According to Chafetz (1990), gender-inequality refers to gender based division of labor, gender social definitions, and power inequalities. Young, Fort, and Danner (1994) define gender inequality as the departure from parity in the representation of women and men in key dimensions of social life. In contrast to the still commonly used concept of women's status, the notion of gender equality points to the dimensions in the distribution of women and men in the central arenas of social life (Young et al., 1994).

The observed variables for gender equality are female-male ratio of mean years of schooling (FMMEAN), political-legal equality for women (POLEQUAL), and social-economic equality for women (SOEQUAL). Female-male ratio of mean years of schooling is calculated by dividing the mean years of schooling among females by the mean years of schooling among males. A coefficient greater than 1 indicates that female mean years of schooling is higher than male mean years of schooling.

The measures of political-legal and social-economic equalities for women are obtained from Humana's *World Human Rights Guide* (1992). The equality measures range from 0 to 3. The number 0 (*NO*) indicates severe violations of freedoms and rights, whereas 1 (*NO*) indicates frequent violations of freedoms and rights. The numeral 2 (*YES*) qualifies otherwise satisfactory answers on the grounds of occasional breaches of respect for freedoms and rights, and 3 (*YES*) represents respect for freedoms and rights.[7]

Population growth is measured by total fertility rate (FERTI) and average annual growth rate (GROWTH). Total fertility rate refers to the number of live births per thousand potentially fertile women (usually 15-44) with regard to a given time period and a given population. Average annual growth of population takes into account total fertility rate, mortality rate, and the rate of immigration.

The dependent dimension is women's reproductive rights (WRR). The word *right* is defined as "something to which one has a just claim" (Webster, 1989, p.1015). Recent international conferences and conventions on human rights, women, and population have referred to reproductive rights as the freedom to decide on the number and spacing of children, information and education in the field, and the right to have control over their bodies. The observed variables of women's reproductive rights in the study are legal abortion right (ABORTION); personal rights to interracial, interreligious, or civil marriages (INTERRAC); personal rights to equality of sexes during marriage and for divorce proceedings (DIVORCE); personal rights to use contraceptive pills and devices (PILLS); and support for distribution of contraceptives (SUPPORT).

The legal status of abortion has three categories: illegal (no exception), legal for medical reasons, and legal for other reasons. The second category "legal for medical reasons" includes "life," "health," and "eugenic." The third category "legal for other reasons" includes "juridical", "socioeconomic", and "on request". Illegal is coded as 0. Each of the reasons in the second category and the first two of the third category are assigned a value of 1. Legal "on request" is coded as 6 because, in countries where abortion is permitted on request, it is also permitted where necessary to protect women's lives or health, and on eugenic, juridical, and socioeconomic grounds (Ross et al., 1993). The level of measurement for the variable, personal rights to interracial, interreligious, or civil marriage, is ordinal. The other two indicators of women's reproductive rights, equality of sexes during marriage and for divorce proceedings, and equality of rights to use contraceptive pills and devices, are measured at the ordinal level. Discrete values in the range 0 to 3 are assigned to the ordinal categories. The number 0 (*NO*) indicates a constant pattern of violations of freedoms and rights; 1 (no) indicates frequent violations of freedoms and rights; 2 (yes) qualifies otherwise satisfactory answers on the grounds of occasional breaches of respect for freedoms and rights; 3 (*YES*) represents respect for the freedoms and rights or guarantees of the article or indicator of the questionnaire.

Support by government for distribution of contraceptives has four categories: 1=major limits, no support; 2=no major limits, no support; 3=no major limits, indirect support; and 4=no major limits, direct support.

Analytical Strategies

The statistical analyses of data are performed to describe the sample data and to test the proposed hypotheses for empirical support. The distributional properties of the variables are examined using several methods such as histograms and box plots. The objective of the descriptive analysis is to determine the current aggregate levels of the proposed correlates of reproductive rights in developing countries. These aggregate levels of the variables provide an empirical understanding of the social and economic context of reproductive rights in developing countries. The variables are described in terms of their geographical variations. An assumption of this study is that developing countries are homogenous with respect to the factors considered. The dissimilarities in the aggregate levels of the variables across geographical regions provide a preliminary test of the validity of the assumption of the geographical homogeneity. The aggregate properties of the variables are examined using frequency distribution, histogram, descriptive statistics, normality, and scatter plot. The analysis of these distributional properties of the variables in combination with examination of multicollinearity and intercorrelations yields information necessary for the selection of the variables.

Frequency distribution The first step in organizing numerically the raw data is to determine the number of valid cases for each observation (Bohrnstedt and Knoke, 1993).

Histogram and boxplot Histograms use bars to represent the frequency, proportion, or percentage of cases associated with each outcome or interval of outcomes of a variable.[8] Histograms are used to identify the properties of frequency distributions. Properties such as unimodality (symmetrical or skewed curves), bimodality (frequency curve has two maxima), and multimodality (frequency curve has more than two maxima) are useful for data description. Boxplot diagrams are used to identify and obtain measures of central tendency and variability. A boxplot readily identifies the median of the distribution. If the median is not in the center of the box, the observed values are skewed. If the median is closer to the bottom of the box than the top, data are positively skewed. If the median is closer to the top than the bottom, data are negatively skewed. The length of the box indicates the extent of the spread or variability of the observations.

Boxplot is also useful in identifying extreme cases. Cases with values more than 3 box-lengths from the upper or lower edge of the box are called *extreme cases* (E). Cases with values between 1.5 and 3 box-lengths from the edge of the box are called *outliers* (O).

Descriptive statistics The properties of variation of the variables are indicated using measures such as standard deviation, skewness, kurtosis, and range. A skewed curve indicates the departure from symmetry of a frequency distribution. A positively skewed curve (longer tail to the right from the central maximum than to the left) indicates an asymmetrical frequency distribution in which larger frequencies are clustered toward the negative end and smaller frequencies toward the positive end. In a negatively skewed distribution (longer tail to the left from the central maximum than to the right), large frequencies are found toward the positive end and small frequencies toward the negative end. Kurtosis measures the degree of peakedness of a distribution (usually taken relative to a normal distribution), leptokurtic (high-peaked), platykurtic (flat-topped), and mesokurtic (not very peaked or flat-topped).

Normality A normal distribution of an observation suggests that 68.27 percent of the cases are included between $\bar{x}-\sigma$ and $\bar{x}+\sigma$, which is one standard deviation on either side of the mean; 95.45 percent of the cases are included between $\bar{x}-2\sigma$ and $\bar{x}+2\sigma$, which is two standard deviations on either side of the mean; and 99.73 percent of the cases are included between $\bar{x}-3\sigma$ and $\bar{x}+3\sigma$, which is three standard deviations on either side of the mean.

Scatter plot and KS significant Scatter plot displays the covariation of two continuous variables as a set of points on a Cartesian coordinate system (Bohrnstedt and Knoke, 1993).

Rules for the selection of the variables The rules for the selection of the variables are based on descriptive statistical properties. To select those that are used for statistical analyses of the study, we look at the following properties of the observation: (a) skewness is less than 1; (b) missing cases for each observation are no more than one third of the observations; (c) unimodal, J-shape, or reverse J-shape are preferred; (d) there are no "E" cases (cases with values more than 3 box-lengths from upper or lower edge of the box); (e) there is normal distribution or close to normal distribution; and (f) the value of KS significant is less than 0.05.

Multicollinearity Correlations among the observed indicators in the study will be used to assess multicollinearity. Very high correlations show the presence of multicollinearity.

Intercorrelations One of the strategies for exploring the validity of the constructs is to examine the intercorrelations among the indicators of the construct.

Structural Equation Analyses

LISREL is used to test the proposed model. Structural equation analysis is basically a multiple regression model using a factor analytical method.[9] When independent variable(s) is (are) measured without error, multivariate least-squares (or maximum likelihood) regression techniques may be used. But when independent variable(s) is (are) assumed to be measured with errors, then the so-called error-in-variables problem arises, and the estimates of the regression coefficients are biased. Measurement error in independent variables tends to attenuate explained variance and standardized regression coefficients. The LISREL model assumes that observed variables are measured with error (Long, 1983a) and facilitates the estimation of measurement error in variables. LISREL provides several measures that assess the overall fit of the proposed model to the covariance structure of manifest variables.

Figure 6.1 shows both the latent and observed variables in the study. The ovals represent the latent variables (factors). They are the underlying theoretical variables of interest. The latent variables are family planning program effort (FPP), socioeconomic development (SOC), secularization (SEC), women's education (WOM), gender equality (GEN), population growth potential (POP), and women's reproductive rights (WRR). The latent factors contribute toward the variance in the observed variables. The variables in boxes are the observed variables. They are family planning program effort scores (PROGRAM), prevalence of contraceptive use (PREVA), human development index (HDI), agriculture as a percentage of GDP (GDPAGR), urban population as a percentage of total (URBAN), percentage of total population in cities with at least 1 million inhabitants (MILLION1), percentage of labor force in agriculture (AGRLAB), percentage of adult literacy (LITER), percentage of adult female literacy (FEMLITER), percentage of females of relevant age enrolled in secondary schools (FEMSEC), female-male ratio of mean years of education (FMMEAN), political-legal equality for women (POLEQUAL), social-economic equality for women (SOEQUAL), total fertility rate (FERTI), annual growth rate (GROWTH), legal abortion right (ABORTION), personal rights to interracial, interreligious, or civil marriages (INTERRAC), personal rights for equality of sexes during marriage and for divorce proceedings (DIVORCE), personal rights to use contraceptive pills and devices (PILLS), and support for distribution of contraceptives and limits to accessibility of contraceptives (SUPPORT).

LISREL has two components: the measurement model and the structural model. The measurement model specifies the relations between the observed and latent variables. The structural model defines the relations among latent factors and the relationship between common factors.

Confirmatory factor analysis Confirmatory factor analysis is used to assess the measurement model. Each of the observed variables loads on a latent factor. Family planning program effort scores and prevalence of contraceptive use load on the latent factor, family planning program effort. Socioeconomic development is measured by the observed variables human development index and agriculture as a percentage of GDP. Secularization is measured by urban population as a percentage of total, percentage of total population in cities with at least 1 million inhabitants, percentage of labor force in agriculture, and percentage of adult literacy. Percentage of female literacy and percentage of females of relevant age enrolled in secondary schools load on women's education. Gender equality has three observed variables: female-male ratio of mean years of schooling, political-legal equality for women, and social-economic equality for women. Population growth is measured by total fertility rate and annual growth rate. Women's reproductive rights are indicated by five variables: legal abortion right; personal rights to interracial, interreligious, or civil marriages; personal rights for equality of sexes during marriage and for divorce proceedings; personal rights to use contraceptive devices; and support for distribution of contraceptives and limits to accessibility of contraceptives.[10]

Structural model The structural portion of the model testing examines the relations among latent variables. There are two types of latent factors, exogenous and endogenous.[11] The exogenous factors in the model are family planning effort, socioeconomic development, and secularization. The endogenous factors are women's education, gender equality, population growth potential, and reproductive rights. The latent factors contribute toward the variance in the manifest variables.

Notes

1. According to Ross, Mauldin, and Miller (1993), 30 indices are employed to obtain family planning programs scores. The indices are grouped into four components. The first component is composed of policies, resources, and stage-setting activities that a government (or a private organization) undertakes to underpin, organize, and implement a family planning program. There are eight items for policy and stage-setting activities. These activities include the setting of population-related policies, especially as regards fertility regulation, funding, and other resources concerning direct provision of family planning supplies and services. These activities also include the involvement of other ministries or government agencies in promoting and providing information about population concerns and family activities, in appointing senior officials to direct family planning programs, and in encouraging private sector populations activities.

The second component is service or service-related activities that are designed to make it easier for people to obtain and use a variety of family planning methods. The items of the second component include information, education, and communication (IE&C) activities; the training of personnel; supervision; community-based distribution of programs; social marketing programs; other service delivery actions; use of civil bureaucracy to underscore the importance of the program and to help carry it out; the providing of incentives for increased use of contraception; the involvement of other ministries or government agencies in providing services or information and education; and clinic-based service delivery systems.

The third component, record keeping and evaluation, consists of three items. They are record keeping, evaluation, and management use of evaluation findings.

The last component refers to the availability and accessibility of contraceptive techniques and devices.

Contraceptive prevalence is estimated on the basis of available survey information. The procedure is described in Mauldin and Ross (1992).

2. A figure of 120 refers to full coverage.

3. The United Nations Development Program (1992) proposed that social and economic development be measured by HDI, which takes into consideration longevity, knowledge, and income. Longevity is measure by life expectancy at birth. Knowledge is measured by two educational stock variables, adult literacy and mean years of schooling. For income, HDI is based on the premise of diminishing returns from income (p.91).

4. Canada has the highest value of HDI (0.982). Japan is ranked 2 (0.981). Three is Norway with HDI 0.978. Switzerland is ranked 4 (0.978). Sweden ranked 5 (0.976). The United States is ranked 6 (0.976). Australia is 7, with HDI of 0.971. France is 8, with HDI of 0.969. Netherlands is ranked 9 (0.968). The United Kingdom is 10, with HDI of 0.962. The country with the lowest HDI is Guinea of Sub-Saharan Africa (HDI=0.052).

5. An illiterate person as defined by UNESCO is a person who cannot read with understanding and write a short and simple statement on his or her everyday life (World Resources Institute, 1992).

6. The United Nations defines "urban agglomeration" as "comprising the city or town proper and also the suburban fringe or thickly settled territory lying outside of, but adjacent to, the city boundaries" (World Resources Institute, 1992).

7. The questionnaires cover 40 indicators from the United Nations treaties, each of which requires answers that are framed into one of the four categories or levels: 3 (*YES*), 2 (yes), 1 (no), and 0 (*NO*).

8. Since the variables used in the study are continuous in feature, an useful type of graph to display the observed values and frequency counts of a frequency distribution is the stem-and-leaf diagram. The diagram resembles a histogram turned on its table.

9. Factor analysis, according to Long (1983a, 1983b), is a statistical procedure for uncovering a (usually) smaller number of latent variables by studying the covariation among a set of observed variables. Or we can say that factor analysis attempts to explain the variation and covariation in a set of observed variables of a ser of unobserved factors.

10. Using exploratory factor analysis, we dropped three observed variables because of their low reliability in relation to the constructs. The dropped variables include the two indicators for secularization (proportion of total tertiary enrollment and technological efficiency) and one indicator for gender equality (female-male gap in labor force).

11. Exogenous latent factors are synonymous with independent variables, and endogenous variables are synonymous with dependent variables.

8   Analyses and Results

This chapter contains four sections. The first section presents the descriptive analyses of the variables. These results provide information to assess distributive properties of the variables. If a variable is highly skewed it may be linearized through logarithmic transformation. This is necessary to ensure the assumptions of normality underlying multivariate analysis for model testing. The second section presents the results of the analysis by geographical regions. The focus of this section is on regional variations on women's reproductive rights. The third section describes the reliability and validity used to measure the latent factors. Measures of association among variables are also presented because they are helpful in making crude assessments of validity of the scales. The final section presents the results of the estimation of the proposed model using structural equation modeling.

Descriptive Statistics

Table 8.1 presents the descriptive statistics for all the variables used in the study. The mean for family planning program effort scores is 50.595, ranging from zero (Kuwait, Libya, and Saudi Arabia) to 100.85 (China); the midpoint falls at 51.935. Contraceptive prevalence in developing countries varies from 0 percent to 80 percent with a mean of 30.789 and median of 28. The standard deviation is high, about 25. The large variation in contraceptive prevalence across nations indicates the large gap in implementing family planning programs in developing countries in spite of its widespread popularity.

Human development index is a measure of socioeconomic development. It varies from a low of 0.052 to a high of 0.927. The mean of HDI is 0.448, and the median is 0.446. Most developing nations have low levels of human development.[1] The variable, agriculture as a percentage of GDP, varies from 3 percent to 72.5 percent. The mean is 25.9, and median is 24.7. These values suggest that most developing countries tend to have a low percentage of agriculture in GDP. Agriculture plays a diminishing role in developing economies today.

The mean value of adult literacy is 64.841 percent, and the median is 66.000. The standard deviation is high, about 24. Most developing countries have achieved high levels of adult literacy. This may be due to the emphasis on literacy through country- and region-wide literacy programs. The mean for urban population as a percentage of the total is 42.6, and the median is 40.4. The mean for the variable, percentage of total population in cities with at least 1 million inhabitants, is about 11.8, and the median is 6.6. Both variables are positively skewed. That is, most developing countries have low levels of urbanization and a low proportion of the population in large cities with at least 1 million inhabitants. The percentage of labor force in agriculture varies from 2 to 93 percent. The mean is 54.755, and the median is 57.500. A high proportion of the population aged 15 to 65 in developing countries is engaged in the agricultural sector.

Table 8.1 Frequencies, means, and standard deviations (N=101)*

Variables	Variable labels	Frequencies	Means	Standard deviations
Program scores	PROGRAM	96	50.695	25.943
Contraceptive prevalence	PREVA	95	30.789	25.245
Human development	HDI	100	0.448	0.255
% agriculture in GDP	GDPAGR	92	25.947	16.976
% urban population	URBAN	100	42.606	23.936
% total population in cities w/at least 1 million inhabitants	MILLION1	98	11.752	16.093
% labor force in agriculture	GARLAB	98	54.755	24.930
% adult literacy rate	LITER	88	64.841	23.938
Adult female literacy rate	FEMLITER	83	53.741	27.195
% female in secondary schools	FEMSEC	96	34.635	25.755
Female-male ratio of mean years of schooling	FMMEAN	99	0.596	0.301
Political-legal equality for women	POLEQUAL	74	1.486	0.602
Socioeconomic equality for women	SOEQUAL	74	1.216	0.476

Table 8.1 Frequencies, means, and standard deviations (N=101) (cont'd.)

Total fertility rate	FERTI	99	5.112	0.725
Average annual growth rate	GROWTH	98	2.597	0.816
Legal abortion right	ABORTION	96	2.053	1.759
Personal rights to interracial, interreligious or civil marriages	INTERRAC	74	2.378	1.003
Personal rights for equality of sexes during marriage and for divorce proceedings	DIVORCE	74	1.527	0.815
Personal rights to use contraceptive pills and devices	PILLS	74	2.878	0.368
Support for distribution of contraceptive devices	SUPPORT	99	3.758	0.624

* Cases with missing values are excluded in this analysis.

The percentage of females enrolled in secondary schools is far lower than the percentage of female adult literates. While adult literacy is high in developing countries, opportunities for females to gain secondary school education remain low.

One of the measures of the gender gap, female-male ratio of mean years of schooling, suggests that males are much more likely to attain a given level of schooling than females. The mean of the variable is 0.596, and the median is 0.580. The variable, political and legal equality for women, has a mean of 1.486, and a median of 2.000. This implies that, generally speaking, in developing countries occasional violations of the freedom and rights are commonplace (Humana, 1992). The level of social and economic equality for women is low. The mean is 1.22, and median is 1.000, with a skewness of 0.590. Women in most developing countries enjoy low levels of social and economic equality although political and legal systems attempt to promote equality for men and women.

Total fertility rate for all developing countries as a whole is 5.112. Women (aged 15 to 44) in developing societies have an average of more than five children. Although annual growth rate varies from 0.15 to almost 4.0, developing nations have an average growth rate of 2.597 percent.

Legal abortion right in developing countries is granted on the basis of health concerns (mean of 2.053 on a 6.0 scale) rather than for socioeconomic reasons or on request. The freedom for interracial, interreligious, or civil marriages is fairly satisfactory with only occasional violations (mean=2.379). Personal rights for equality of sexes during marriage and for divorce proceedings are not as satisfactory as intermarriage rights (Humana, 1992). The mean of 1.527 and median of 2.000 suggest that equality between men and women for marriage and divorce is often not granted. The mean of the variables, personal rights to use contraceptive pills and devices, is 2.878, and the median is 3.0. The mean of the variable, support for distribution of contraceptives and limits to accessibility of contraceptives, is 3.758, and the median is 4.0. The skewness of both variables is negative. This indicates that few restrictions are imposed on contraceptive use in most developing nations.

The descriptive analyses of the variables in the hypothesized model reveal several notable characteristics of developing nations. Family planning programs vary largely in terms of the effort scores and contraceptive prevalence. Family planning program effort scores tend to be higher in comparison with contraceptive use, which points to the need to improve the efficiency of family planning programs. Developing countries have high rates of fertility and low levels of socioeconomic development and urbanization. However, the percentage of agriculture in GDP is found to be low for most nations, which implies to the processes of industrial and economic development in developing countries. Most countries in the developing world have a high percentage of adult literacy, while the proportion of females enrolled in secondary schools is low.

In terms of women's reproductive rights, personal rights to use contraceptives and support for contraceptive distribution are found to be satisfactory. This implies that family planning programs aiming at lowering fertility have gained wide popularity both in practice and government policies. Personal rights for intermarriages and equality during marriage and for divorce proceedings are found to be frequently violated. Meanwhile, in most developing countries, legal abortion is permitted only on life and health grounds rather than for social and economic considerations.

Regional Variations in Women's Reproductive Rights

Developing countries are classified into four regions. Sub-Saharan Africa, Latin America/Caribbean, Middle East/North Africa, and Asia are recognized as broad homogeneous cultural groups (World Bank, 1994b). The analyses are conducted in four stages. At the first stage, the variations in women's reproductive rights are assessed within each region. In the second stage, the variations across regions on each of the four indicators of reproductive rights are examined.[2] The third stage examines the regional variations by clustering nations with similar reproductive rights scores. At the fourth stage, multiple regression analysis is used to explore the effects of regions on women's reproductive rights net of the controls. Mean substitutions are used to replace missing data.

Variations of women's reproductive rights within regions In terms of the levels of legal abortion right, Asian countries, as a whole, have the highest level compared with the other regions. Legal abortion right is granted in most Asian countries on socioeconomic grounds. Populations of China, Korea (Democratic), Malaysia, Mongolia, Singapore, and Vietnam enjoy complete freedom for legal abortion right. In this region abortion is illegal only in Nepal. Middle East/North Africa registers a slightly higher level of legal abortion right than Sub-Saharan Africa and Latin America/Caribbean. In most nations in Middle East/North Africa, legal abortion right is granted for health or eugenic reasons. While abortion is granted on request in Tunisia and Turkey, Oman requires that abortion be illegal with no exceptions. Legal abortion right in most countries in Latin America/Caribbean is granted based on life and health considerations. Five out of 24 countries in the region consider abortion illegal (Chile, Columbia, Dominican Republic, Honduras, and Paraguay).

Sub-Saharan Africa as a whole registers a slightly higher level of legal abortion right than Latin America/Caribbean. Abortion is illegal in Liberia and Zaire, whereas legal abortion right is granted for both medical and juridical concerns in Kenya, Lesotho, Mozambique, South Africa, Tanzania, and Zimbabwe.

Latin America/Caribbean enjoys the highest level of personal rights to interracial, interreligious, or civil marriages compared with the other regions. Middle Eastern and North African countries have the lowest level of intermarriage rights. Severe violations of the rights can be found in most countries in the region. The majority of the countries in Sub-Saharan Africa grant the rights for interracial, interreligious, or civil marriages with the exception of Sudan, where the rights appear to be severely violated. In Asia, only three countries have a low level of personal rights. They are Afghanistan, Bangladesh, and Pakistan.

In terms of personal rights of sexes for equality during marriage and for divorce proceedings, the Latin America/Caribbean region scores the highest in comparison with the other regions. Asian and Sub-Saharan African nations grant men and women similar levels of equality during marriage and for divorce proceedings. Occasional violations are found in most of the countries in the region. Severe violations of the rights are found in Sudan, Afghanistan, and Pakistan. The lowest level of personal rights for equality of sexes during marriage and for divorce proceedings is found in countries in Middle East/North Africa, where the rights are often severely violated. Women in Iran, Kuwait, Morocco, Saudi Arabia, and Yemen do not enjoy equal rights for marriage and divorce.

Asia, Latin America/Caribbean, and Sub-Saharan Africa offer full-fledged support for contraceptive distribution; one exception is Gabon in Africa, with no restriction but no government support. Countries in Middle East/North Africa have low levels of support for contraceptive distribution. There is no support for contraceptive distribution in Saudi Arabia.

Variations of women's reproductive rights across regions The levels of legal abortion right (1989 and 1992) in developing countries vary from region to region. Figure 8.1 shows that Asian countries had the highest level of legal abortion right in both 1992 and 1989, and the level of abortion right increased slightly in 1992. This may be due to the fact that in Asian countries legal abortion right was more available on juridical grounds in 1992 than in 1989. Middle East/North Africa registered a slightly higher level of legal abortion right in 1992 and 1989 than Sub-Saharan Africa and Latin America/Caribbean. In most nations in Middle East/North Africa, legal abortion (1989, 1992) right was granted only for health or eugenic reasons. Figure 8.1 also shows that abortion right in countries of Latin America/Caribbean declined from a mean of 2.25 in 1989 to a mean of 1.571 in 1992.

Figure 8.2 shows the regional variations in personal rights for equality of sexes during marriage and for divorce proceedings. The Latin America/Caribbean region scores the highest. The mean (2.095) indicates that the equality of sexes during marriage and for divorce proceedings in countries in Latin America/Caribbean is favorably high, but marriage laws and traditional beliefs still favor husbands. Asian and Sub-Saharan African nations have similar levels of equality during marriage and for divorce proceedings (mean=1.4 for Africa; mean=1.526 for Asia). The mean levels of personal rights for equality of sexes during marriage and for divorce proceedings of the two regions are low. This may be due to the fact that personal rights for equality during marriage and for divorce proceedings in Sub-Saharan African and Asian countries are occasionally violated. The lowest level of personal rights for equality of sexes during marriage and for divorce proceedings is found in countries in Middle East/North Africa (mean=0.857), where the rights for equality in marriage and for divorce are often severely violated.

The three regions of Sub-Saharan Africa, Latin America/Caribbean, and Asia enjoy similar levels of personal rights to use contraceptive devices and pills. Occasional violations of the rights are found in some countries in Middle East/North Africa.

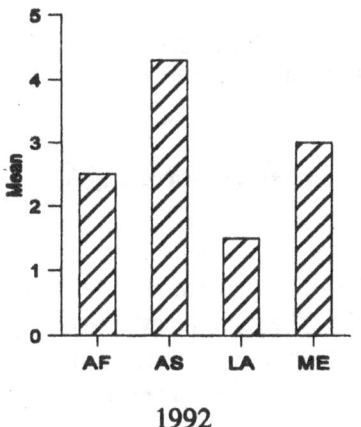
1992

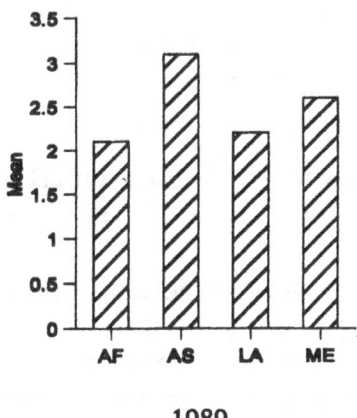
1989

AF: Sub-Saharan Africa LA: Latin America/Caribbean
AS: Asia ME: Middle East/North Africa

Figure 8.1 Mean comparison of legal abortion right in 1992 and 1989

78 *Women's Reproductive Rights in Developing Countries*

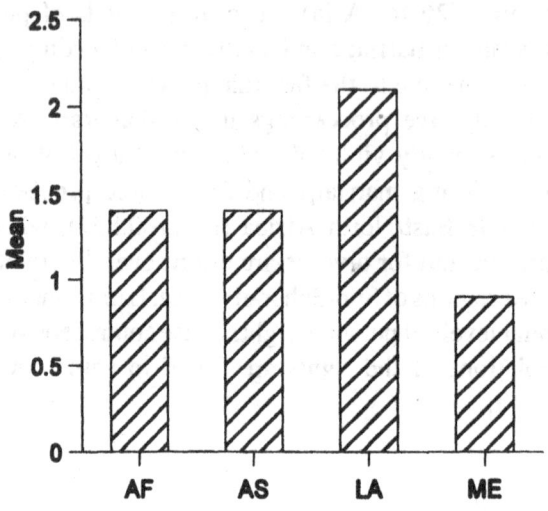

AF: Sub-Saharan Africa
AS: Asia
LA: Latin America/Caribbean
ME: Middle East/North Africa

Figure 8.2   Mean comparison of marriage and divorce rights

In Latin America/Caribbean region freedom of interracial, interreligious, or civil marriages is fully respected (Figure 8.3). The region registers the highest level of personal rights for interracial, interreligious, or civil marriages in comparison with the other three regions. These rights are severely violated in Middle East/North Africa.

Figure 8.4 presents the regional comparisons in reproductive rights scores. These scores are obtained by combining the two factor score scales, legal abortion right and personal rights. The highest scores are found in Latin American countries (score mean=0.514). Africa and Asia have similar scores, 0.238 and 0.183, respectively. The Middle East/North Africa region scores the lowest with a mean of -1.347.

Regional variations in reproductive rights scores are divided into low (-2.336 to -1.129), medium (-0.828 to 0.379), and high (0.548 to 1.79). Sixty-three percent of the countries in Middle East/North Africa have low scores, while

63 percent of the countries in Africa have medium reproductive rights scores. Latin America accounts for over half of the countries that have high reproductive rights scores, while the Middle East has only 25 percent of the countries with high scores.

Cluster analysis Another approach for describing the variations in reproductive rights across nations is by clustering nations with similar levels of reproductive rights. A cluster analysis technique is used to cluster nations with similar values on the four indicators of reproductive rights, legal abortion right, intermarriage rights, divorce and remarriage rights, and the right to use contraceptives.

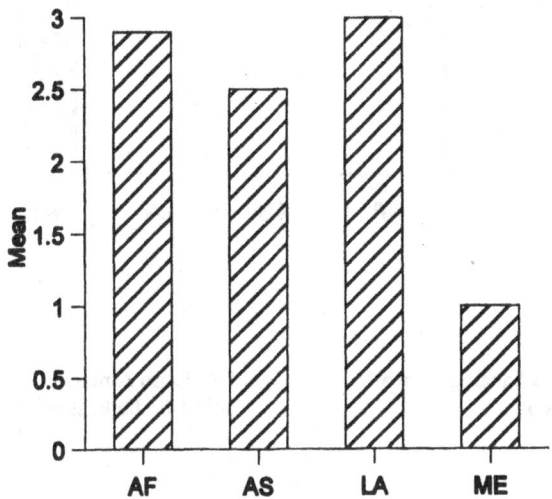

AF: Sub-Saharan Africa LA: Latin America/Caribbean
AS: Asia ME: Middle East/North Africa

Figure 8.3   Mean comparison of civil and intermarriage rights

80 Women's Reproductive Rights in Developing Countries

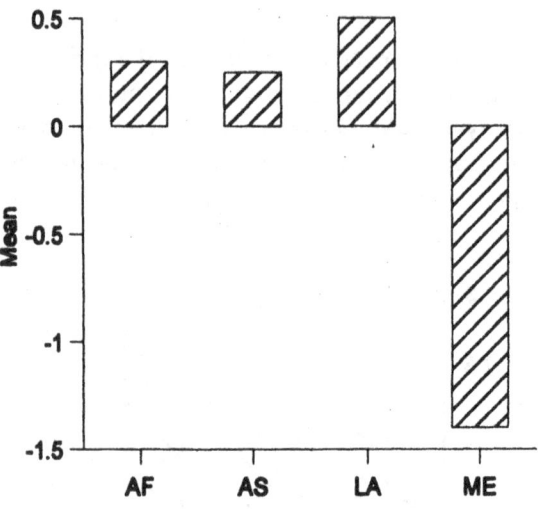

AF: Sub-Saharan Africa LA: Latin America/Caribbean
AS: Asia ME: Middle East/North Africa

Figure 8.4   Regional comparison of reproductive rights scores

Table 8.2 Reproductive rights: a cluster analysis of developing nations (N=74)

Cluster	Nations	Cluster	Nations	Cluster	Nations
1	Togo (F); Malaysia (A); India (A)	2	Libya (M); Oman (M); Kuwait (M); Saudi Arabia (M); Iran (M); Afghanistan (A); Yemen (M); Pakistan (A); Morocco (M); Syria (M); Tunisia (M); Algeria (M); Jordan (M); Egypt (M)	3	Sierra Leone (F); Guatemala (L); Malawi (F); Trinidad and Tobago (L); Philippines (A); Chile (L); Honduras (L); Peru (L); Columbia (L); Dominican Republic (L); Jamaica (L); Paraguay (L); Nepal (A); Bolivia (L); Papua New Guinea (A); Botswana (F); Senegal (F); Zaire (F); Rwanda (F); Uganda (F); Nigeria (F)
4	Zambia (F); Thailand (A); Indonesia (A); Tanzania (F); Zimbabwe (F); Mozambique (F); Niger (F); Argentina (L); El Salvador (L); Hong Kong (A); Korea (R) (A); Kenya (F)	6	Korea (D) (A); Vietnam (A); Cuba (L); Ghana (F); Singapore (A); China (A)		
5	Iraq (M); Turkey (M); Costa Rica (L); Ecuador (L); Benin (F); Brazil (L); Cameroon (F); Panama (L); Uruguay (L)				
7	Myanmar (A); Venezuela (L); Sudan (F); Mexico (L); Sri Lanka (A); Angola (F); Nicaragua (L); Bangladesh (A); South Africa (F)				

Notes: F = Africa; L = Latin America/Caribbean; M = Middle East/North Africa; A = Asia.

Table 8.2 presents the clusters of nations generated by using the hierarchical cluster analysis technique. Of the 101 countries, 28 are excluded due to missing data. Seven clusters are formed at the third stage of clustering, using the nearest neighborhood approach. The second cluster is comprised mostly of Middle East/North African countries. The third cluster is represented almost equally by Latin American and Sub-Saharan African nations. Of the 21 nations in the third cluster, 11 are Latin American and eight are Sub-Saharan African. The fourth cluster is a mixture of Asian and Sub-Saharan African countries. Progressive Sub-Saharan African states, such as Zambia and Zimbabwe, share similar reproductive rights levels with the fast-developing Asian nations, such as Hong Kong and Thailand. Of the nine nations in the fifth cluster, five are Latin American and two are Sub-Saharan African countries. In general, Middle East/North African countries have similar levels of reproductive rights, and a large proportion of Latin American and Sub-Saharan African states have similar levels of reproductive rights. Approximately half the Asian nations in the analysis are in the cluster labeled *other*. The rest of the Asian nations are distributed across the first three clusters. Very broadly, we suggest that there are three types of clusters: Asian, Middle Eastern, and Latin American/Sub-Saharan African.

Multiple regression analysis Table 8.3 presents the estimates of the effects of region variables, annual growth rate (Growth), family planning program effort scores (Program), adult literacy rate (Literacy), human development index (HDI), percentage of urban population (Urban), social-economic equality for women (Equality), and percentage of Muslims and Roman Catholics (Muscat) on abortion right.

The first equation contains the three region dummies and all the independent variables except for religion. The reference category for the region dummies is Latin America/Caribbean. Three regions are significantly different from the Latin America/Caribbean region with respect to the level of legal abortion right. These three regions possess significantly higher levels of legal abortion right than the Latin America/Caribbean region. None of the independent variables in the equation is statistically significant. The strength and significance levels of the variables are not altered when the variable religion is added to the equation (Equation 2). The addition of religion does not modify the significance level of the region dummies. Thus, regional variations in legal abortion right remain even when variables of socioeconomic development, family planning program effort, gender equality, and religion are controlled for.

Table 8.3 Unstandardized and standardized coefficients for OLS additive models of legal abortion right (standardized coefficients in parentheses)

	Equation 1		Equation 2	
Variables	ß	Variables		ß
Africa	1.030**	Africa		1.068**
	(0.504)			(0.523)
Middle-East	0.813**	Middle-East		0.830**
	(0.298)			(0.304)
Asia	1.170**	Asia		1.212**
	(0.485)			(0.503)
Growth	-0.128	Growth		-0.131
	(-0.102)			(-0.106)
Program	0.003	Program		0.003
	(0.079)			(0.079)
Literacy	0.005	Literacy		0.005
	(0.102)			(0.102)
HDI	0.520	HDI		0.543
	(0.132)			(0.138)
Urban	0.004	Urban		0.004
	(0.089)			(0.087)
Equality	0.297	Equality		0.301
	(0.121)			(0.123)
Constant	-1.658	Muscat		0.056
				(0.028)
		Constant		-1.712
Multiple R = 0.417		Multiple R = 0.418		
$R^2 = 0.174$		$R^2 = 0.175$		

** $p<0.01$.

Table 8.4 Unstandardized and standardized coefficients for OLS additive models of personal rights (standardized coefficients in parentheses)

	Equation 1		Equation 2
Variables	ß	Variables	ß
Africa	0.206	Africa	0.038
	(0.101)		(0.041)
Middle-East	-1.321**	Middle-East	-1.375**
	(-0.485)		(-0.505)
Asia	-0.140	Asia	-0.276
	(-0.058)		(-0.115)
Growth	0.175	Growth	-0.162
	(0.140)		(-0.130)
Program	0.005	Program	0.005
	(0.124)		(0.126)
Literacy	0.010**	Literacy	0.010**
	(0.217)		(0.218)
HDI	-0.127	HDI	-0.200
	(-0.032)		(-0.051)
Urban	0.002	Urban	0.002
	(0.040)		(0.047)
Equality	0.546**	Equality	0.534**
	(0.222)		(0.217)
Constant	-0.945	Muscat	-0.181
			(0.091)
		Constant	-0.771
Multiple R = 0.748		Multiple R = 0.752	
$R^2 = 0.560$		$R^2 = 0.566$	

** $p < 0.01$.

Table 8.4 presents the estimates of the effects of the independent variables on personal rights. The mean level of personal rights score of Middle Eastern/North African nations is significantly lower than that of the personal rights scores of the Latin American/Caribbean region. Among the remaining variables, literacy and gender equality have significant and positive effects on personal rights scores. The strength and significance levels of the variables are not altered when the variable religion is added to the equation. The mean personal rights score of the Middle East remains significantly lower than the Latin American/Caribbean mean personal rights score. This regional difference is neither diminished nor changed by the addition of the variable of religion.

The results of the multiple regression analysis strongly suggest the presence of significant regional variations when several selected social-structural variables are taken into account. Furthermore, the regional variations in legal abortion right are extensive than the variations obtained in personal rights across regions.

Measurement Model

This section shifts the focus of analysis to evaluating the adequacy of the measurement model. Thus far, the analysis focused on several selected measures of dimensions such as gender equality and women's education. Descriptive analysis of the variables provides the information about the distributional properties of the selected variables. This information is crucial in making decisions with respect to appropriate statistical transformations that are necessary for variables which violates normal distributional properties assumed. At a substantive level, arguments were presented to justify the selection of the indicators associated with the key dimensions of fertility, women's education, etc. The next step is to explore the empirical support for the substantive claims that have been made. For example, variables such as, abortion rights, rights to divorce, and contraception rights were selected as indicators to measure women's reproductive rights. The empirical support for this and similar claims are assessed in the course of evaluating the measurement model.

Table 8.5   Correlations among indicators within constructs

Family planning program effort (FPP)					
	PROGRAM	PREVA			
PROGRAM	1.000				
PREVA	0.631*	1.000			
Socioeconomic development (SOC)					
	HDI	GDPAGR			
HDI	1.000				
GDPAGR	-0.694*	1.000			
Secularization (SEC)					
	URBAN	MILLION1	AGRLAB	LITER	
URBAN	1.000				
MILLION1	0.641*	1.000			
AGRLAB	-0.766*	-0.560*	1.000		
LITER	0.430*	0.280*	-0.491*	1.000	
Women's education (WOM)					
	FEMLITER	FEMSEC			
FEMLITER	1.000				
FEMSEC	0.660*	1.000			
Gender equality (GEN)					
	FMMEAN	POLEQUAL	SOEQUAL		
FMMEAN	1.000				
POLEQUAL	0.375*	1.000			
SOEQUAL	0.401*	0.488*	1.000		
Population growth (POP)					
	FERTI	GROWTH			
FERTI	1.000				
GROWTH	0.776*	1.000			
Women's reproductive rights (WRR)					
	ABORTION	INTERRAC	DIVORCE	PILLS	SUPPORT
ABORTION	1.000				
INTERRAC	0.070	1.000			
DIVORCE	0.170	0.641*	1.000		
PILLS	0.000	0.350*	0.289*	1.000	
SUPPORT	0.130	0.370*	0.130	0.419*	1.000

* $p < 0.05$.

Measures of Association Table 8.5 presents the correlations among all the variables in the hypothesized model. The correlation coefficient between family planning program effort scores (PROGRAM) and contraceptive prevalence (PREVA) is 0.631, which suggests a positive and strong relationship between the variables. The degree of human development (HDI) and the percentage of agriculture in GDP (GDPAGR) are negatively related to each other (-0.694). Percentage of urban population (URBAN) is positively correlated with proportion of population in cities of more than 1 million inhabitants (MILLION1) (0.641), but it is negatively related to proportion of labor force in agriculture (AGRLAB) (-0.776). Proportion of labor force in agriculture is found to be negatively associated with adult literacy (LITER) (-0.491).

The correlation between female literacy rate (FEMLITER) and percentage of females of relevant age enrolled in secondary schools (FEMSEC) is positive (0.660). The relationship between political-legal equality for women (POLEQUAL) and social-economic equality for women (SOEQUAL) is positive and moderately strong (0.488). Political-legal and social-economic equality for women is found to have a positive association with female-male ratio of mean years of schooling. The correlation coefficients are 0.375 and 0.401, respectively. This suggests that at high levels of political-legal and social-economic equality for women, women are more likely to pursue educational goals. Total fertility rate is found to have a positive relationship with annual growth rate (0.776).

In terms of women's reproductive rights, personal rights for interracial, interreligious, or civil marriages are positively associated with equal rights during marriage and for divorce proceedings. The correlation coefficient is 0.641. Personal rights to use contraceptives are positively related to support for contraceptive distribution (0.419).

A high level of correlation among the variables that are related theoretically to the constructs demonstrates convergent validity (Carmine and Zeller, 1979; Cook and Campbell, 1979). An examination of the correlations among variables associated with each of the hypothesized seven constructs supports the presence of convergent validity of the scales (see Table 8.5). The correlations are, in general, strong and significant. The indicators of women's reproductive rights are poorly correlated. In particular, the right to legal abortion does not have significant correlations with the other indicators.

The intercorrelations among the seven factors are presented in Table 8.6. Most of the intercorrelations are moderate and significant. The absence of strong intercorrelations among factors indicates that the factors may be adequately discriminated from one another.

The measurement model consists of the relations between the observed (indicators) and unobserved (latent) variables.[3] Confirmatory factor analysis is used to estimate the parameters of the measurement model. Table 8.7 presents the confirmatory factor analysis results. It should be noted that these estimates are net estimates. All the constructs in the hypothesized model are estimated simultaneously.

In this study, factors are assigned a scale for measurement. Each latent factor shares a scale of 1 with one of its indicators. That is, one of the indicators is assigned a loading of value 1. The estimates (ML) of all factor loadings are high and significant. In addition to factor loadings, squared multiple correlations (SMC) are used to estimate the reliability of the observed variables in relation to the constructs. The value of SMC for family planning program effort scores (PROGRAM) is 0.901, which indicates that about 90 percent of the variance in family planning program effort scores may be accounted for by the latent factor, family planning program effort, controlling for the other factor. The second indicator for family planning effort is contraceptive prevalence (PREVA). About 47 percent of the variance in this variable is accounted for by the latent factor controlling for effort scores. The dimension of socioeconomic development explains about 90 percent of the variance in human development (HDI) and about 55 percent of the variance in GDP (GDPAGR).

Table 8.6 Intercorrelations among constructs in the reproductive rights model

	1	2	3	4	5	6	7
1	0.425*						
2	0.475*	0.880*					
3	0.340*	0.732*	0.687*				
4	0.414*	0.743*	0.584*	0.603*			
5	0.360*	0.544*	0.425*	0.547*	0.593*		
6	-0.536	-0.622*	-0.459*	-0.600*	-0.530*	0.913*	
7	0.106*	0.041	0.003	0.084	0.244*	-0.129	0.169*

* $p < 0.05$.
1 = Family planning program effort; 2 = Socioeconomic development;
3 = Secularization; 4 = Women's education; 5 = Gender equality;
6 = Population growth; 7 = Women's reproductive rights.

Table 8.7 Measurement model parameters for women's reproductive rights (standardized solutions in parentheses)

Variables				Variables			
Latent	Observed (X-variables)	Slope (SMC)	R^2	Latent	Observed (Y-variables)	Slope (SMC)	R^2
FPP	PROGRAM	1.00(0.954)	0.901	WOM	FEMLITER	1.000(0.942)	0.899
	PREVA	0.721**(0.688)	0.468		FEMSEC	0.900**(0.848)	0.711
SOC	HDI	1.000(0.959)	0.902	GEN	FMMEAN	1.000(0.953)	0.901
	GDPAGR	−0.776**(−0.745)	0.549		POLEQUAL	0.529**(0.504)	0.251
					SOEQUAL	0.558**(0.532)	0.280
SEC	URBAN	1.000(0.954)	0.901	POP	FERTI	1.000(0.954)	0.901
	MILLION1	0.715**(0.682)	0.460		GROWTH	0.853**(0.813)	0.655
	AGRLAB	−0.922**(−0.880)	0.766	WRR	ABORTION	1.000(0.351)	0.122
	LITER	0.566**(0.540)	0.289		INTERRAC	2.624**(0.921)	0.839
					DIVORCE	1.930**(0.677)	0.454
					PILLS	1.176**(0.413)	0.169
					SUPPORT	1.385**(0.486)	0.234

** $p < 0.01$.
FPP: Family planning program effort; SOC: socioeconomic development; SEC: Secularization; WOM: Women's education; GEN: Gender equality; POP: Population growth; WRR: Women's reproductive rights.

Of the four indicators of secularization, two have high R squared values. They are URBAN and AGRLAB. The other two indicators have moderate to low R squared values. In particular, the R squared value of LITER is low, about 0.30. The two indicators of women's education, FEMLITER and FEMSEC, have high R squared values, indicating adequate levels of reliability. The R squared value of FEMLITER is about 0.90, and that of FEMSEC is 0.71.

Among the observed variables of gender equality (FMMEAN, POLEQUAL, SOEQUAL) two indicators, POLEQUAL and SOEQUAL, are found to have low levels of reliability. The R squared value of POLEQUAL is 0.25, and that of SOEQUAL is 0.28.

Total fertility (FERTI) and annual growth rate (GROWTH) are reliable indicators of population growth potential, with R squared values of 0.901 and 0.655, respectively. Among the indicators of women's reproductive rights, personal rights to interracial, interreligious, or civil marriages (INTERRAC) is the most reliable indicator. About 84 percent of the variance in this variable is accounted for by women's reproductive rights controlling for the other four indicators. About 45 percent of the variance in the indicator DIVORCE is accounted for by women's reproductive rights controlling for the other indicators. ABORTION and SUPPORT have low R squared values, 0.17 and 0.23 respectively. These two indicators will be retained for substantive reasons even though they have low reliability values.[4]

The confirmatory factor analysis results provide reasonable empirical evidence of the construct validity of the proposed latent traits that are hypothesized to influence the selected indicators.

Structural Model and Test of the Hypotheses

The structural portion of the model consists of the relations among latent variables. Structural model specifies the hypothesized relationships among constructs in the model. The empirical findings provide partial support for population growth explanation. Table 8.8 presents the unstandardized and standardized parameter estimates of the structural model. The model proposes a negative impact of population potential on women's reproductive rights. The relationship is not significant at the 0.05 level. No empirical support is found to support the hypothesis. Of the four background factors that influence population growth, three are found to be statistically significant. The empirical findings support the hypothesis that family planning program effort reduces

92 *Women's Reproductive Rights in Developing Countries*

population growth. Socioeconomic development has a negative effect on population growth. Furthermore, gender equality leads to fertility decline.

The estimated relationship between women's education and reproductive rights is found to be significant but negative. The empirical findings support the hypothesis that women's education increases the level of gender equality (P<0.01). Socioeconomic development has a positive effect on women's education, as hypothesized. However, secularization is not significantly associated with women's education. Of the four hypotheses associated with women's education, two are supported.

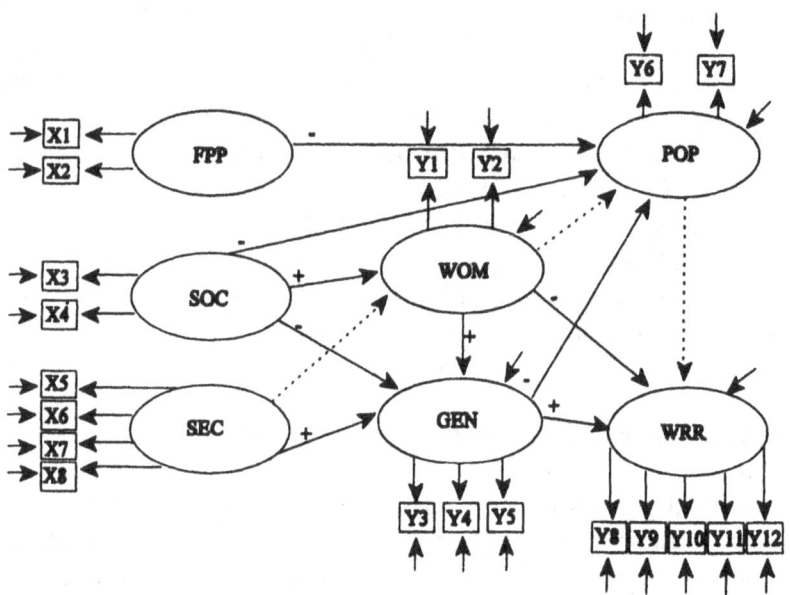

Figure 8.5 Reduced model of women's reproductive rights

Note: See Table 6.1 for variable definition. Exogenous variables are interrelated.

Gender equality is significantly related to women's reproductive rights, as hypothesized. Socioeconomic development in developing countries is found to have a significant and negative effect on gender equality. Secularization has a significant and positive effect on gender equality. Figure 8.5 presents the reduced model with the significant paths.

Decomposition of the total causal effects among the exogenous and endogenous factors is presented in Table 8.9. Gender equality has a strong direct effect on women's reproductive rights. The direct effect is 0.705. The total effect of gender equality on reproductive rights is 0.643. Family planning program effort has a negative effect on population growth. The total effect is -0.455. Socioeconomic development has a strong and negative effect on population growth (total effect, -0.513). The effect of gender equality on population growth is -0.481. The decomposition of causal effects indicates strong and negative effects of family planning program effort, socioeconomic development, and gender equality on population growth.

The direct effect of women's education on reproductive rights is found to be strong and negative (-0.870). Although there is a strong and positive indirect relationship between the variables, the total effect is very weak. Women's education has a strong and direct positive effect on gender equality. Socioeconomic development has a strong and positive effect on women's education. The total effect of socioeconomic development on women's education is 0.894.

The results from the decomposition of causal effects indicate that both direct and total effects of gender equality on women's reproductive rights are strong and positive. Socioeconomic development has a strong but negative effect on gender equality. The direct effect of socioeconomic development on gender equality is -0.930. The total effect of socioeconomic development on gender equality, however, is weak due to a strong and positive indirect effect. Both secularization and women's education are found to have strong and positive effects on gender equality.

Table 8.8 Structural model, LISREL estimates (maximum likelihood), unstandardized and standardized parameter estimates (standardized estimates in parentheses)

	Exogenous factors		Endogenous factors	
	WOM	GEN	POP	WRR
FPP	--	--	-0.314** (-0.319)	--
SOC	0.894** (0.869)	-0.930** (-0.904)	-0.760** (-0.773)	--
SEC	-0.089 (-0.086)	0.509** (0.495)	--	--
WOM	--	1.175** (1.176)	0.3420 (0.293)	-0.730** (-1.208)
GEN	--	--	-0.481** (-0.502)	0.706** (1.167)
POP	--	--	--	0.129 (0.205)

** $p < 0.01$.

Table 8.9 Decomposition of causal effects

Variables and paths	Direct	Indirect	Total
POP - WRR	0.129	--	0.129
FPP - POP	-0.314	-0.141	-0.455
SOC - POP	-0.761	0.248	-0.513
WOM - POP	0.333	-0.556	-0.223
GEN - POP	-0.481	--	-0.481
WOM - WRR	-0.870	0.800	0.070
SOC - WOM	0.894	--	0.894
SEC - WOM	-0.089	--	-0.089
WOM - GEN	1.175	--	1.175
GEN - WRR	0.705	-0.062	0.643
SOC - GEN	-0.930	1.050	0.120
SEC - GEN	0.510	-0.105	-0.405

Overall Model Fit The assessment of empirical support for each of the proposed hypotheses is often accompanied by the assessment of the fit of the overall model to data. The overall model fit is assessed as follows. A simple method of detecting misspecification of latent trait models involves the use of Q plot. Q Plot is a graph of the normalized residuals (Figure 8.6).

When residuals are distributed along the diagonal of the Q-plot graph, the model may not be misspecified. The residual from the estimated model that appears to deviate away from the diagnosis suggests a misspecified model.

LISREL provides fit statistics and information about the adequacy of the model. The most frequently used measure is the likelihood-ratio chi-square statistics (Joreskog and Sorbom, 1989). Chi-square tests are used to determine whether the differences between the predicted variance-covariance matrix and the actual variance-covariance matrix approach zero. A statistically significant chi-square indicates a statistically significant discrepancy between the data (variance-covariance matrix) and the model (variance-covariance matrix implied from the maximum likelihood parameter estimates). When the hypothesized model perfectly fits the data, chi-square will be small in relation to the degrees of freedom (df). A chi-square measure that is statistically insignificant indicates a good fit of the model to the data.[5]

96 *Women's Reproductive Rights in Developing Countries*

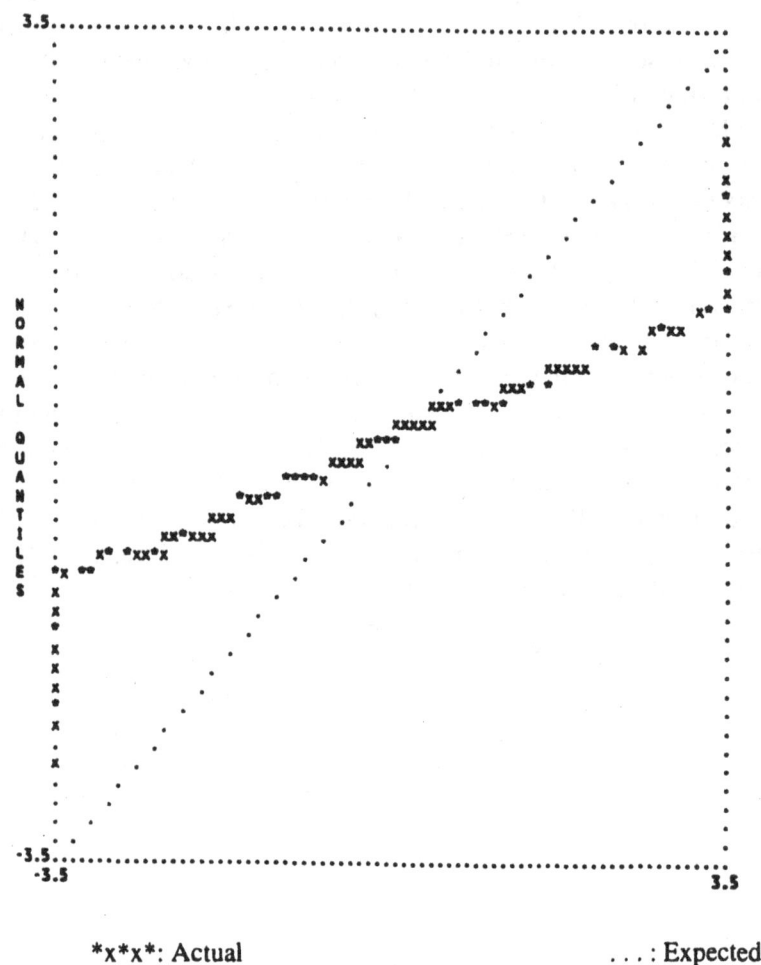

*x*x*: Actual   . . . : Expected

Figure 8.6   Women's reproductive rights: Q-plot of standardized residuals

Table 8.10 shows that the chi-square is 679.18 (df=165) for the proposed model of women's reproductive rights. The ratio of chi-square and degrees of freedom is 4.12. The value is less than 5.

The goodness of fit index (GFI) and adjusted goodness of fit (AGFI) are used to estimate model fit. GFI measure is not affected by sample size and is robust against departure from normality (Lavee, 1988). Theoretically, GFI ranges from 0 to 1. A value closer to 1 indicates a better model fit. A small difference (less than 0.05) between GFI and AGFI also indicates that the model fits well to the data. The GFI and AGFI values are 0.617 and 0.512 for the proposed model. The difference between GFI and AGFI does not suggest that the proposed model of women's reproductive rights adequately fits the data.

The fourth measure of model fit is the root mean square residual (RMSR). It is a measure of the mean discrepancy between data and the implied variances and covariances. It represents the average deviation of the predicted from the actual correlation matrix. The lower the index, the better the fit of the model to the data. RMSR is 0.173 for the proposed model. This value is much higher than the desirable values of RMSR below 0.05. Generally speaking, Q-Plot, chi-square statistics, GFI, AGFI, and RMSR, considered together, indicate that the overall fit of the model to the data is not satisfactory.

The lack of fit of the proposed models with the data presents an opportunity to build on the proposed models. A crucial step in this regard consists of assessing the stability of the model against disturbances in the composition of the sample itself. Sample size may be disturbed by randomly dropping a country from the sample. The proposed model may be reestimated using the sample (reconstituted) from which a country has been randomly dropped. The similarity among estimates obtained from the several reconstituted samples considerably increases the confidence in the model estimates obtained. This strategy was adopted by dropping a country randomly four times with replacement. The proposed model was reestimated four times using the reconstituted samples. All four reestimations produced similar parameter estimates. There were no changes in the direction and significance level of the estimates. The changes in the magnitude of the parameters were small. The model estimates from the four separate sample trials were correlated. The correlations among the distributions of estimates fell within a narrow range of 0.7 to 0.85.[6]

Table 8.10   Overall model fit indices

Goodness of fit index (GFI)	0.617
Adjusted goodness of fit index (AGFI)	0.512
Root mean square residual (RMSR)	0.173
Chi-square	679.18
Degrees of freedom (df)	165
Total coefficient of determination for X-variables	0.991
Total coefficient of determination for Y-variables	0.995
Coefficient of determination for structural equations	0.931

Table 8.11 presents research hypotheses and empirical findings. The empirical findings from the structural equation modeling indicate that gender equality is a crucial factor that brings about women's reproductive rights in developing countries. Family planning program effort and socioeconomic development have a negative effect on population growth. Socioeconomic development increases the attainment of women's education. Secularization has a positive effect on women's education, and women's education is found to have a positive effect on gender equality. There are three unexpected findings. First, women's education has a strong and negative effect on reproductive rights. Secondly, the relationship between women's education and population growth is not statistically significant. Finally, socioeconomic development in developing countries is negatively associated with gender equality. These findings are perhaps suggestive of the variation in the effects of variables on women's reproductive rights brought about by the complex influences of modernization on the lives of women in developing countries.

Table 8.11 Research hypotheses and empirical findings

Hypotheses	Significance
Population growth has a negative effect on women's reproductive rights	Not
Family planning program effort has a negative effect on population growth	Sig. -
Socioeconomic development has a negative effect on population growth	Sig. -
Women's education has a negative effect on population growth	Not
Gender equality has a negative effect on population growth	Sig. -
Women's education has a positive effect on women's reproductive rights	Sig. -
Women's education has a positive effect on gender equality	Sig. +
Socioeconomic development has a positive effect on women's education	Sig. +
Secularization has a positive effect on women's education	Not
Gender equality has a positive effect on women's reproductive rights	Sig. +
Socioeconomic development has a positive effect on gender equality	Sig. -
Secularization has a positive effect on gender equality	Sig. +

Notes

1. The United Nations Development Program (1992) divided the human development index into three categories, high, medium, and low. For high human development, HDI is 0.800 or above; for medium level of human development, HDI values are between 0.500 and 0.799; and for low human development, HDI weighs below 0.500.

2. Four observed variables of women's reproductive rights are chosen for regional variation analyses. The variables are abortion right; personal rights to interracial, interreligious, or civil marriages; personal rights for equality of sexes during marriage and for divorce proceedings; and personal rights to use contraceptive pills and devices.

3. The measurement model specifies the pattern by which observed measures load onto a particular factor.

4. To determine whether the presence of these indicators results in changes in the values of the measurement model parameters, the measurement model is reestimated after dropping three indicators, PILLS, POLEQUAL, and SOEQUAL. The values of factor loadings and R-squared values of the variables in the two measurement models are similar.

5. The ratio of chi-square to degree of freedom is sometimes cited as an indication of model fit. A chi-square/df ratio of less than 5 is often regarded as an indication of model fit. Chi-square statistics is sensitive to sample size. According to Lavee (1988), the model is more likely to be "fit" when a small sample is used. Chi-square statistics assumes multivariate normality, which is difficult to assess. With these limitations, Joreskog and Sorborn (1989) suggest alternative ways in addition to chi-square/df ratio to assess model fit.

6. A number of post hoc modeling approaches are available to increase the model fit. The approach is adopted in the next chapter. The study intends to test the theoretical explanations. To this end, the focus is on the estimation of the structural parameters of the model rather than achieving a best fit model.

9 Post Hoc Modeling of Women's Reproductive Rights

We have so far adapted the traditional approach to theory building. This approach involved explicit predictions of relationships among social factors based on substantive theories. The empirical tests of the proposed model yielded only partial support for the model. We now attempt to search for a model with more predictive validity than the model which was empirically tested. The sample data can be explored to discover empirical relationships. These relationships may be incorporated into the theoretical model. The revised model is likely to yield a better fit to the data. This process of discovering models which fit the data is called post hoc modeling. Several pieces (submodels) of the theoretical model of reproductive rights are examined separately. We attempt to improve these submodels. The submodels are integrated to obtain a post hoc model of reproductive rights.

This chapter contains three sections. The first section describes the empirical findings for an alternative model. The second section examines the submodels of women's reproductive rights. The third section presents cumulative probit models of the indicators of women's reproductive rights.

Alternative Model Testing

It is hypothesized that the most important determinant of women's reproductive rights is population growth. It is proposed that gender equality and women's education have both direct and indirect effects on women's reproductive rights through population growth, with modernization factors as background variables. Empirical tests of the proposed model provide no support for the hypothesized relationship between population growth and women's reproductive rights.

Is it possible that women's reproductive rights influence population growth? As women gain the power to make reproductive decisions, they are more likely to use contraception and voluntarily reduce family size. In order to explore this possible alternative, the direction of the causal arrow from population growth to women's reproductive rights in the proposed model is reversed (Figure 9.1).

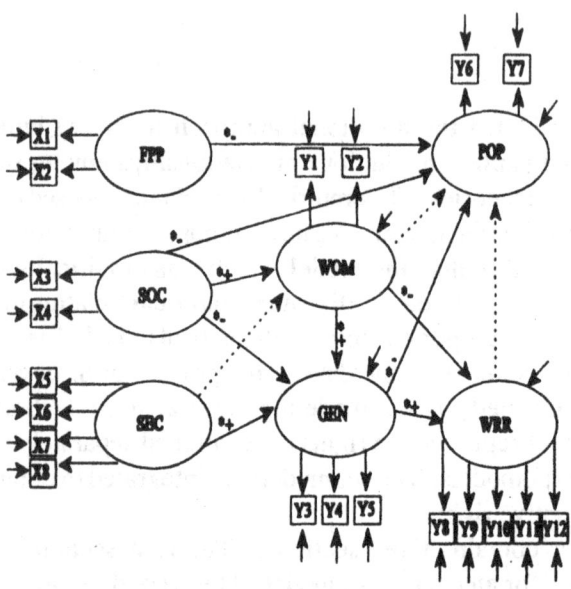

Figure 9.1   The alternative model of women's reproductive rights: the effect of reproductive rights on population growth

Note: See Table 6.1 for variable definitions. Exogenous factors are interrelated.

This model is evaluated using structural equation modeling methods. The empirical findings indicate that the path from women's reproductive rights to population growth is not statistically significant. The results suggest that the effect of population growth and family planning program effort on women's reproductive rights is insignificant. The improvement of women's reproductive rights does not necessarily lead to a decline in population growth rate in developing countries (see Table 9.1).

Tests of Submodels

We now proceed to evaluate a submodel after dropping family planning program effort and population growth from the proposed model of women's reproductive rights. This is done in two stages. First, the submodel of causal associations among the proximate determinants of women's reproductive rights, gender equality, and women's education are evaluated using LISREL (see Figure 9.2).

The effect of women's education on women's reproductive rights is negative and statistically significant. Gender equality has a positive significant effect on women's reproductive rights. Furthermore, women's education has a positive effect on gender equality. These results correspond to the results obtained from the evaluation of the proposed model in chapter 8.

Table 9.1 The alternative model, LISREL estimates (maximum likelihood), unstandardized and standardized parameter estimates (standardized estimates in parentheses)

Exogenous factors	WOM	GEN	POP	WRR
WOM	-	-	-0.342**(-0.347)	-
SOC	0.892**(0.864)	-0.981**(-0.947)	-0.689**(-0.699)	-
SEC	-0.083(-0.081)	0.535**(0.517)	-	-
Endogenous factors				
WOM	-	1.200**(1.197)	0.279(0.293)	-0.809**(-1.312)
GEN	-	-	-0.499**(-0.524)	0.684**(1.112)
POP	-	-	-	-
WRR	-	-	0.109(0.070)	-

** $p < 0.01$.

104 *Women's Reproductive Rights in Developing Countries*

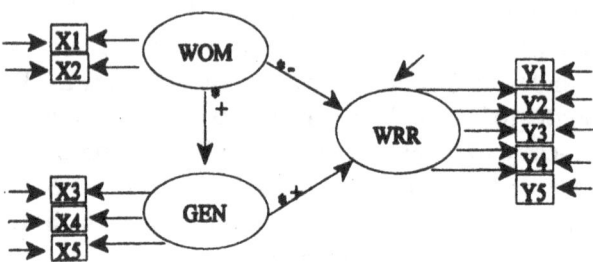

Figure 9.2   Women's reproductive rights: a submodel of proximate factors

Note: See Table 6.1 for variable definitions.

At the second stage, the submodel of women's reproductive rights is extended by adding background factors, socioeconomic development (SOC), and secularization (SEC). The causal associations between background variables and the intervening factors, gender equality (GEN) and women's education (WOM), from the proposed full model are maintained (Figure 9.3).

The two sets of estimates are compared. The first set of estimates is obtained from the estimation of the submodel of women's reproductive rights. The second set of estimates is obtained from the estimation of the expanded model of women's reproductive rights. Table 9.2 presents the comparison of the two sets of estimates. The results suggest that the addition of the background variables does not alter the effects of women's education and gender equality on reproductive rights. Women's education has a negative and significant effect on reproductive rights. Gender equality has a positive and significant effect on women's reproductive rights. The relationship between women's education and gender equality is positive and significant.

The relationship between socioeconomic development and women's education remains positive and significant. Secularization, however, is found to have no significant effect on gender equality. This finding is dissimilar to the estimated positive and significant relationship between secularization and gender equality (see Table 8.8). The results also indicate that the negative relationship between socioeconomic development and gender equality found in the proposed model does not exist in the expanded submodel.

The role of secularization in predicting reproductive rights levels appears to be insignificant. A more parsimonious model of women's reproductive rights involving one background factor, socioeconomic development, and two intervening factors, gender equality and women's education, is proposed (Figure 9.4).

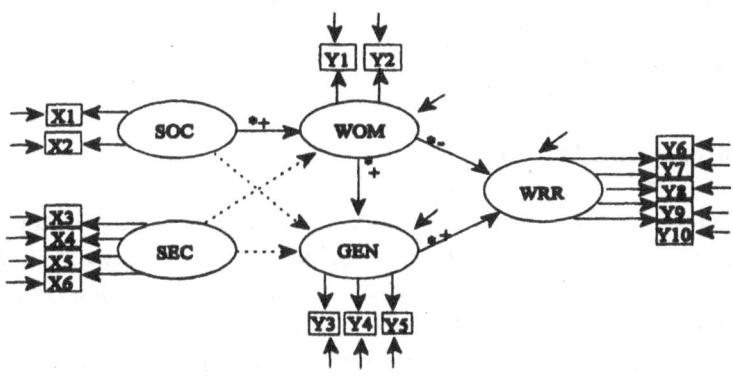

Figure 9.3 Women's reproductive rights: expansion of the submodel

Note: See Table 6.1 for variable definitions. Exogenous factors are interrelated.

Table 9.2 Submodels, LISREL estimates (maximum likelihood), unstandardized and standardized parameter estimates (standardized estimates in parentheses)

Exogenous factors		Endogenous factors	
		Submodel	
	WOM	GEN	WRR
WOM	-	0.348**(0.614)	-0.525**(-0.552)
GEN	-	-	1.855**(1.106)
		Expanded submodel	
SOC	2.462*(2.566)	-1.299(-1.359)	-
SEC	-1.109(-1.155)	0.680(0.711)	-
WOM	-	1.587**(1.593)	-0.280*(-0.826)
GEN	-	-	0.561* (1.648)

* $p < 0.05$.
** $p < 0.01$.

Cumulative Probit Modeling

In arriving at a parsimonious model of women's reproductive rights, three determinants are selected. They are socioeconomic development, gender equality, and women's education. Women's reproductive rights are indicated by ABORTION, INTERRAC, DIVORCE, PILLS, and SUPPORT. All these indicators are measured at an ordinal level, as was reported in chapter 7.

It is plausible that the effects of the three selected determinants on each of the five indicators of reproductive rights differ. Path analytic methods provide a simple strategy to assess the causal effects of the determinants on each of the five indicators of reproductive rights. However, since the dependent variables are measured at ordinal level, it is not appropriate to use ordinary least square (OLS) unless interval level measurement of the dependent variable is assumed. It is more appropriate to use logit regression method.

A logit modeling approach is used. The analysis is done in three stages. In the first stage, the variable FEMLITER (female literacy rate) is selected as an appropriate indicator of women's education. POLEQUAL (political-legal equality for women) is selected as an indicator of gender equality, and HDI (human development index) is used to indicate socioeconomic development. In addition, AGRLAB (percentage of labor force in agriculture) is used as a control variable. This caution is used to address the fact that agricultural societies are more likely to have a reduced level of female literacy and gender equality. In the second stage, a cumulative probit model is analyzed for each of the five indicators of reproductive rights.

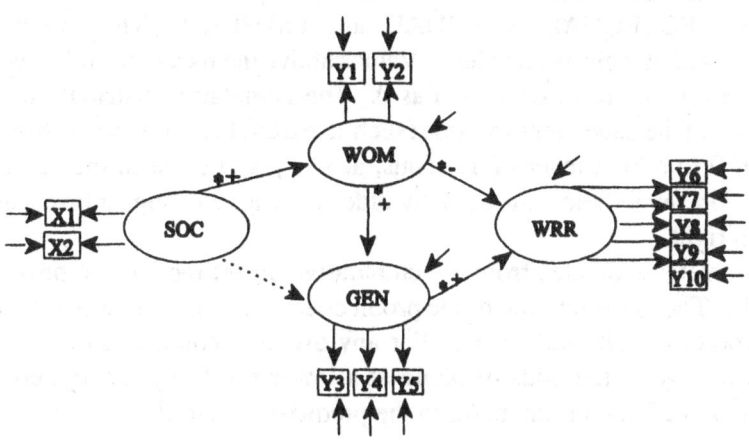

Figure 9.4   Women's reproductive rights: reassessed version of the expanded submodel

Note: See Table 6.1 for variable definitions.

Cumulative probit distributions facilitate the retention of the ordinal properties of the dependent variable. The legal status of abortion has three categories: illegal (no exception), legal for medical reasons, and legal for other reasons. The second category, legal for medical reasons, includes life, health, and eugenic. The third category, legal for other reasons, includes juridical, socioeconomic, and on request. Illegal is coded as 0. Each of the second and the first two of the third categories are coded as 1. On request is coded as 6. The three categories are arranged ordinally, with higher numerical values indicating more liberal levels of legal abortion right.

The other three indicators of women's reproductive rights, INTERRAC, DIVORCE, and PILLS, are measured at ordinal level. Discrete values in the range of 0 to 3 are assigned to the ordinal categories. Higher numerical values indicate more liberal levels of rights to enter into marriage and for equality during marriage and for divorce proceedings. The last indicator of women's reproductive rights, SUPPORT, has four categories (1-4). High values indicate high levels of government support.

The independent variables in the cumulative probit model are FEMLITER, FEMSEC, POLEQUAL, SOEQUAL, and FMMEAN. The variables are dichotomized at their mean values. Values above the mean are coded as 1, and values below the mean are coded as 0. The cumulative distributions of the categories of the dependent variable (such as ABORTION) cumulate from a low value of 0 to a high level of 1. Thus, at any given point in the cumulative distribution, levels below the point include countries with higher levels of legal abortion right.

Parameter estimates from the cumulative probit models are provided in Table 9.3. The interpretation of the probit coefficients is similar to the method of interpreting logit coefficients. For any dividing point, $100 (e^b - 1)$ is the percent change in the odds of being at a lower level than being above that dividing point for a unit increase in the predictor variable.

Table 9.3 Cumulative probit models for ABORTION, INTERRAC, DIVORCE, PILLS, and SUPPORT

Variables	ABORTION		INTERRAC		DIVORCE		PILLS		SUPPORT	
	odds ratio	S.E	odds ratio	S.E.	odds ratio	S.E.	odds ratio	S.E.	odds ratio	S.E
Percentage of Adult Female Literacy	34.92** (3392)	0.495	10.59** (959)	0.352	1.28 (28)	0.334	8.04** (904)	0.421	7.85* (685)	0.322
Percentage of females relevant age enrolled in Secondary Schools	2.01 (101)	0.371	0.09** (-91)	0.371	0.75 (-25)	0.313	1.08 (8)	0.364	0.78 (-22)	0.371
Female-Male ratio of mean years of schooling	0.75 (-25)	0.429	1.60 (60)	0.398	3.92+ (292)	0.370	0.33 (-67)	0.479	2.82+ (182)	0.291
Political & legal equality for woman	1.91 (91)	0.267	25.46** (2446)	0.290	5.08** (408)	0.254	18.08** (1708)	0.323	4.650+* (365)	0.284
Social & economic equality for woman	2.25+ (125)	0.264	1.11 (11)	0.245	26.63** (2563)	0.271	0.06** (-94)	0.306	16.73* (1573)	0.261

** $p < 0.01$; * $p < 0.05$; + $p < 0.1$.
Values in parenthesis show the percentage change in odds ratio.

Two variables, FEMLITER and POLEQUAL, have significant positive effects on each of the five indicators of reproductive rights except for DIVORCE. The magnitude of the effect of these two variables is greater than the effects of the remaining predictors in the model. The variable SOEQUAL is also an important predictor. Those nations that have a higher proportion of literate adult females than the average proportion for all developing countries are more likely to have liberal rights for marriage and divorce. The percentage change in the odds is high, about 96 percent. Most variables do not have significant effects on legal abortion right.

In order to test the stability of the coefficients, we introduced region variables. It is argued that rights are determined by the cultural characteristics of nations. In order to control for the cultural context, several region dummies are added. There are four categories of developing regions: Sub-Saharan Africa, Latin America/Caribbean, Middle East/North Africa, and Asia (World Bank, 1994b). The Asian region is the reference group. The dummies are added to the predictors in the cumulative probit model. Table 9.4 provides the results for the cumulative probit modeling for ABORTION, INTERRAC, DIVORCE, PILLS, and SUPPORT, controlling for regions. POLEQUAL and FEMLITER persist as the most important predictors in each of the five models.

In the third stage we assessed a path model in which HDI influences FEMLITER and FEMLITER influences POLEQUAL. In addition, HDI influences POLEQUAL. This model adequately retains the causal associations of the parsimonious model that resulted from structural equation analysis of data. Furthermore, it incorporates the results from the estimation of cumulative probit model estimates. It is found that FEMLITER and POLEQUAL are important predictors.

The directions and levels of significance of the paths are shown in Figure 9.5. In these diagrams, we have fused the results we obtained from the evaluation of probit models and path models. The empirical findings from the path analysis correspond to the findings from the structural equation analysis that women's reproductive rights in developing countries are affected by the structural changes resulting from modernization processes.

Table 9.4 Cumulative probit models for ABORTION, INTERRAC, DIVORCE, PILLS, and SUPPORT controlling for regions

Variables	ABORTION odds ratio	S.E	INTERRAC odds ratio	S.E.	DIVORCE odds ratio	S.E.	PILLS odds ratio	S.E.	SUPPORT odds ratio	S.E.
Percentage of Adult Female Literacy	5.98** (498)	0.498	2.730* (173)	0.391	0.770 (-23)	0.362	2.550* (155)	0.448	2.420+ (142)	0.421
Percentage of females relevant age enrolled in Secondary Schools	1.130 (13)	0.444	0.95** (-5)	0.469	1.630 (63)	0.388	0.840 (-16)	0.468	0.600 (-40)	0.441
Female-Male ratio of mean years of schooling	1.22 (22)	0.444	1.830 (83)	0.463	2.490* (149)	0.427	0.580 (-42)	0.507	0.550 (-45)	0.483
Political & legal equality for woman	1.660+ (66)	0.309	5.29** (429)	0.332	1.910* (91)	0.273	3.66** (266)	0.339	3.380* (238)	0.313
Social & economic equality for woman	1.39 (39)	0.292	0.580+ (-42)	0.303	4.59** (359)	0.280	0.29** (-71)	0.333	0.180* (-82)	0.331
Africa	0.45* (-55)	0.415	3.22** (222)	0.419	1.030 (3)	0.373	0.530 (-47)	0.444	0.500 (-50)	0.403
Latin America	0.13** (-87)	0.375	2.350+ (135)	0.485	0.600+ (-40)	0.314	0.800 (-20)	0.399	0.750+ (-25)	0.378
Middle East	0.51 (-49)	0.495	0.11** (-89)	0.529	0.27** (-73)	0.485	0.550 (-45)	0.515	0.420 (-58)	0.495

** p<0.01; * p<0.05; + p<0.1.
Values in parenthesis show the percentage change in odds ratio.

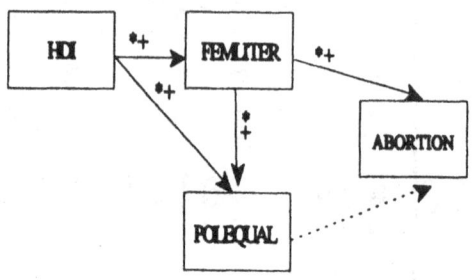

Figure 9.5a Path model of legal abortion right

Note: See Table 6.1 for variable definitions.

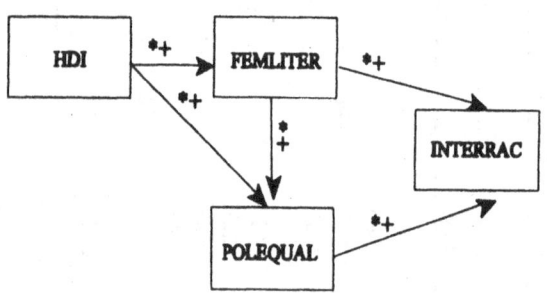

Figure 9.5b Path model of personal rights to interracial, interreligious, or civil marriages

Note: See Table 6.1 for variable definitions.

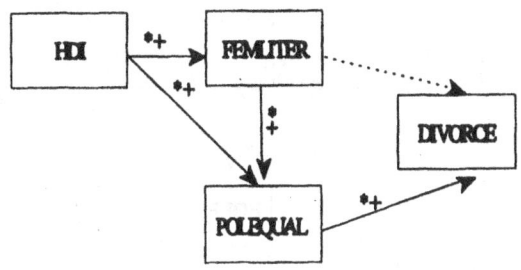

Figure 9.5c   Path model of personal rights for equality of sexes during marriage and for divorce proceedings

Note: See Table 6.1 for variable definitions.

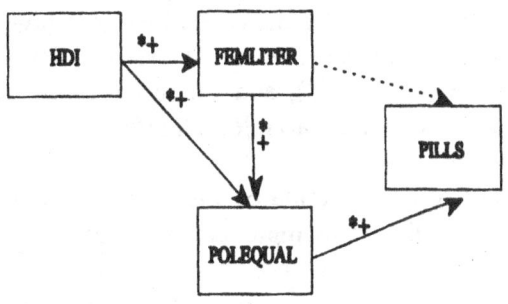

Figure 9.5d   Path model of personal rights to use contraceptive pills and devices

Note: See Table 6.1 for variable definitions.

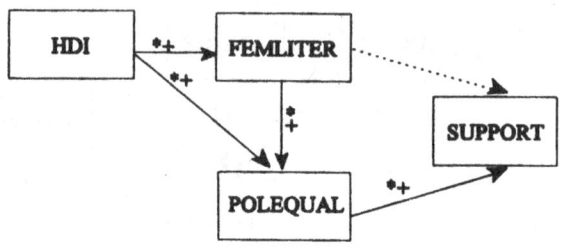

Figure 9.5e   Path model of support for contraceptive use

Note: See Table 6.1 for variable definitions. *p<.1

The path coefficients indicate a positive effect of FEMLITER on legal abortion right (ABORTION). Gender equality does not affect abortion right (Figure 9.5a). In terms of personal rights to intermarriages and the use of contraceptives, women's education (FEMLITER) and gender equality (POLEQUAL) exert significant and positive effects (Figure 9.5b). FEMLITER does not have a significant effect on equal marriage and divorce rights (DIVORCE). Higher levels of gender equality lead to higher levels of marriage and divorce rights for women (Figure 9.5c), personal rights to use contraceptive pills and devices (Figure 9.5d), and support for contraceptive distribution (Figure 9.5e). The exogenous variable HDI influences women's education and gender equality.

The findings from the cumulative probit models and path models suggest that the processes leading to an improvement in each of the five components of women's reproductive rights are not uniform in every respect in relation to the structural changes due to modernization. Personal rights to civil or intermarriages and contraceptive use are affected by women's education and gender equality for women brought about by socioeconomic development. Personal rights for equality of sexes during marriage and for divorce proceedings are found to be affected by gender equality. Women's education is not related to marriage and divorce rights. Higher levels of women's education, however, lead to higher levels of legal abortion right in developing countries.[1]

Note

1. Gender equality (POLEQUAL) is found to have no significant relationship with abortion right.

10   Discussion and Conclusion

Women's reproductive rights emerged as a key political and social policy issue in the very recent times. It owes its increasing conspicuousness to population control, human rights movements, and growing concerns about women and their reproductive health. Following the adoption of the Convention on the Elimination of All Forms of Discrimination against Women (CEDAW) (1979) (Appendix E), the World Conference on Human Rights (1993), the International Conference on Population and Development (1994), and the Fourth World Conference on Women (1995) (Appendix F) have contributed to the international recognition of the importance of women's reproductive rights.

The issue of women's reproductive rights is also a particularly controversial topic (United Nations, 1996). Women's reproductive rights touch on matters that are inextricably tied to social and cultural values. The international debates on reproductive rights involve issues that are political, philosophical, and ideological. At the core of the controversy are the top-down family planning programs in developing countries and the recent concern about women's personal rights and reproductive health.

World population is projected to increase by one third between 1990 and 2010 (Dixon-Mueller, 1993). International concerns about the adverse effects of rapid population growth on economic development and environmental degradation, especially in developing countries, have been expressed in world conferences and conventions on population and development. Family planning programs oriented toward finding a quick solution to population problems by focusing on quantitative objectives have aroused controversy because of human rights abuses. On the other hand, women's health advocates and scholars who press for the protection of individual autonomy demand a shift in focus from providing contraception to reproductive health. The nature of the relationship between population growth, economic development, and reproductive rights is a subject of current interest among policy makers and academicians.

This study tests a theoretical model of women's reproductive rights in relation to family planning programs and modernization processes in developing nations. It is argued, that variations in reproductive rights may be accounted for by broad social changes which are likely to reduce fertility and increase the levels of women's education and gender equality. These trends are seen as resulting from broad societal transformations brought about by economic development and secularization. In addition, anti-natalistic population policies in developing countries in the late 20th century provides a strong state-sponsored social control over total fertility rate which may contribute to the attainment of women's reproductive rights.

Summary

Population Control and Women's Reproductive Rights One of the components of the concept of women's reproductive rights is the right of access to methods, information, and education concerning family planning. Reproductive rights are defined as the rights of couples and individuals to decide freely and responsibly the number and spacing of children, the right to have the information and means to do so, and the right to have control over their bodies. The theoretical model proposes that family planning program effort has a negative effect on population growth, which is hypothesized as the most proximate determinant of reproductive rights. Both gender equality and women's education are expected to influence reproductive rights through population growth.

The findings from 101 developing countries suggest that family planning programs in developing countries reduce population growth. The findings also suggest that the relationship between population growth and reproductive rights is statistically insignificant. According to WHO (1986), the right of access to contraceptive methods, information, education, and means of family planning should include the following components. The first is the physical access; that is, are contraceptives available to women who want to use them? The second component relates to the informed consent on the part of the users; that is, are women adequately informed of the properties and the side effects of the contraceptive methods? The third component refers to the ultimate aim of family planning programs which should be aimed at insuing women's autonomy for reproductive decision-making and improving women's reproductive health rather than reaching quantitative goals only. One of the major recommendations of the international conferences on women and human rights (1993, 1994, 1995) is that family planning programs should guarantee the attainment of the highest standard of sexual and reproductive health.

Discussion and Conclusion   119

Gender Equality and Women's Reproductive Rights Structural changes due to modernization processes are hypothesized to influence women's reproductive rights. The impact of socioeconomic development on women's reproductive rights is transmitted through women's education and gender equality.

The empirical findings from both the proposed model (Figure 6.1) and the submodels (Figures 9.2 and 9.3) indicate that socioeconomic development has a significant and positive effect on women's education. The trajectories of modernization in many ways increase women's educational attainment. Secularization has a significant and positive effect on gender equality. The relationship between women's education and gender equality is significant and positive. Gender equality has a strong and positive effect on women's reproductive rights (see Figure 8.5).

The findings considerably increase the importance of gender equality, as it remains the only proximate determinant of reproductive rights with a positive effect. The results from the test of the submodels reaffirm the positive effect of gender equality in achieving women's reproductive rights. Forces which shape egalitarian structures are of importance. The findings that gender equality is the most important component in the model supports Dixon-Mueller's (1993) argument that the social structure of the opportunities that women face in society is a crucial determinant of women's reproductive rights.

Women's Education and Reproductive Rights The empirical findings indicate that women's education is negatively related to reproductive rights. The reason for the negative relationship is not immediately apparent. It may suggest a complex relationship among economic development, women's education, and reproductive rights. Economic development is likely to provide more opportunities for women to pursue their education. While women in developing nations gain higher levels of education as a result of the processes of modernization, it is not necessarily true that an increase in women's education will lead to more reproductive rights. It is possible that women's capital may not automatically be translated into social and political advantages to enact legislation and protect their reproductive rights. It may be conjectured that women's education has only discretionary value during early stages of economic development. Education may be more instrumental in achieving marital mobility than in acquiring personal rights. This finding may suggest a critical approach to social policies to facilitate structural changes and address social equality for both sexes. Malhotra et al. (1995) state that, while women in most societies gain higher levels of education as a result of socioeconomic development, improvement in women's education may not result in reproductive rights if gender inequality prevails.

Regional Variations in Women's Reproductive Rights The effect of culture on women's reproductive rights is one of the pervasive areas of investigation in the reproductive rights literature. Four regions, Sub-Saharan Africa, Latin America/Caribbean, Middle East/North Africa, and Asia, are recognized as broad homogeneous cultural regions. The empirical findings suggest that these regions vary in the levels of women's reproductive rights.

The descriptive analysis of regional variations suggests that the Asian region enjoys a higher level of legal abortion right than the rest of the regions. During 1989 and 1992, almost all regions except for Latin America/Caribbean experienced improvements in abortion right. The Latin America/Caribbean region possesses the lowest level of legal abortion right. In spite of this low ranking in abortion right, the region enjoys a higher ranking than the rest on personal right to civil or intermarriages and personal rights for equality during marriage and for divorce proceedings. The Middle East/North African region has the lowest level of personal rights to civil or intermarriages and personal rights for equality during marriage and for divorce proceedings. Legal abortion right in the Middle East/North African region appears to be more liberal than personal rights to intermarriages and rights for equality of sexes during marriage and for divorce proceedings.

Almost 63 percent of the countries in Middle East/North Africa have low reproductive rights scores. The homogeneity among the Middle East/North African nations with respect to personal rights and abortion right is further supported by the formation of the Middle East/North African cluster in the course of cluster analysis procedures.

The OLS estimates of the region dummies in general support the results from the descriptive analysis of the data. The three regions, Asia, Middle East/North Africa, and Sub-Saharan Africa, possess significantly higher levels of legal abortion right than the Latin America/Caribbean region. Furthermore, the mean personal rights score of the Middle East/North African nations is significantly lower than that score of the Latin America/Caribbean region.

These results from regional variation analysis have several policy implications. Since the regional variations in legal abortion right are well pronounced, cross-regional equality in abortion right may be hard to achieve. Studies are needed to comprehend the source of the cross-regional variation. The controls such as percentage of Muslims and Roman Catholics in the regression model are insignificant. These control variables do not successfully account for the variations in legal abortion right. Several alternative models are to be developed to further account for the regional variations.

There is a marked homogeneity with respect to the levels of personal rights to intermarriages and personal rights for equality of sexes during marriage and for divorce proceedings. Only one region, the Middle East/North Africa, is significantly different from the rest. This difference could not be accounted for by factors such as religion. International policies should focus on strategies for improving women's control over mate selection and the equality of sexes during marriage and divorce.

In sum, policies are immediately needed to reduce the wide regional variations in legal abortion right and to address the special cultural and social forces in the Middle East/North African region that may restrict women's rights to marriage and the rights for equality of sexes during marriage and for divorce proceedings.

Policy Implications

The fundamental importance of reproductive rights for human welfare is often unrecognized for several reasons. First, the concept of reproductive rights remains defined and articulated in egoistic terms. Second, the social and cultural factors which shape the extent of rights remain unspecified at the theoretical and policy levels. Third, the human meaning and definition of reproductive rights tend to be value and cultural specific. For these reasons, empirical research on reproductive rights may invoke fears of conflict between the values of the investigator and the values pertaining to reproductive rights of the local people (Dixon-Mueller, 1993).

The empirical findings from this study throw some light on a few long-standing issues and social policies with regard to the role of economic development and population control policies on women's lives.

Population Control Policies in Developing Countries should Promote Women's Reproductive Rights and Reproductive Well-being The empirical findings suggest that family planning programs have a significant and negative effect on population growth, but the relationship between population growth and reproductive rights is statistically insignificant. Despite the popularity and controversies of family planning programs, current population control policies in some developing countries have failed to promote women's reproductive rights and reproductive well-being. The finding that population growth is not significantly related to reproductive rights supports the claims made by a large number of non-governmental organizations and women's groups at the Cairo conference that success of population policies should not be limited to a narrow sphere of family size reduction. The stewardship model partially condones sacrifices of basic civil and political rights of women in the name of economic progress.

For more than four decades, economic development has been prescribed for fertility decline and women's emancipation. However, current experiences with development, especially in some developing countries, suggest that economic development engenders and maintains traditional ideologies which limit women's access to resources on a par with men (Clark, 1994). Family planning programs and population control policies should promote women's reproductive rights and reproductive well-being (Pearson and Sweetman, 1994). Setting an agenda for the international community to address women's reproductive rights and reproductive health in population control policies is of immediate importance.

International and National Policy Makers Should Take Gender Dimensions into All Projects and Programs The empirical findings from this study point to the crucial importance of gender equality in the model of women's reproductive rights. Berheide and Chow (1994) argue that social policies which emphasize both the micro- and macro- structural gender equalities are important. According to the United Nations (1995), progress in changing discriminatory institutions in some developing countries remains slowest in the area of family laws. The rights to marriage, divorce, custody, and inheritance to control and own property are still problematic. In some Asian, Middle-Eastern, and African countries where the government is influenced by the Islamic religion, grounds for divorce can be different between women and men (United Nations, 1995). Family laws in many developing countries still reflect traditional social and cultural expectations, beliefs, and norms that favor men.

Article 15 of the Convention on the Elimination of All Forms of Discrimination Against Women (CEDAW) accords women equality with men before the law. The Nairobi Forward-looking Strategies (see Appendix C) called for reforms to guarantee women's constitutional and legal rights in terms of access to political, legal, social, and economic resources. In reality, however, women in some developing countries do not have the opportunity to exercise legal capacity on the same basis as men, even where the laws exist (United

Nations, 1995). The review and appraisal for the advancement of women of the United Nations (1995) report that, for women in many countries, the legal autonomy envisaged in the Nairobi Forward-looking Strategies has not been achieved in every aspect of life. Because of persisting inequalities in gender relations and constraints posed by the sexual division of labor in both public and private spheres, structural adjustment policies in many countries have rendered women especially vulnerable. Structural adjustment policies have not sufficiently incorporated gender- and country-specific issues (United Nations, 1995). The lag of gender awareness both at the conceptual and implementation levels, together with methodological and theoretical difficulties has failed to produce gender-sensitive development policies.

Women for a New Era (1990) in its five-year agenda addressed women's reproductive rights and population along with economic structures and environment as important channels to gender equality. The Women's Declaration on Population Policies and DAWN's Population Policies and Reproductive Rights Project emphasized that the empowerment of women and women's health are goals in their own right. A conscious effort on the part of the national and international policy makers to take gender dimensions into all projects and programs is needed.

There are three major dimensions that are closely related to gender equality: equal access to resources including education, employment, and health care; autonomy, that is, the freedom to make decisions on every aspect of life choices; and power, that is, equal participation and ability in the making of decisions (Agassi, 1989; Dunn, Almquist and Chafetz, 1993; Ferree and Hall, 1996). Gender differentials in the extent of access to employment are reflected in the feminization of the labor force and high female unemployment rates.

> If the distribution of women's employment is considered by seven major occupation groups, professional and technical, administrative and managerial, clerical, sales, services, agriculture, and production, it can be noted that women are concentrated in clerical, services and professional and technical occupations. In Chile, where women made up 30.5 percent of the labor force in 1991, they represented 51.3 percent of service workers. ... Country differences persist in the extent of feminization of many clerical and service jobs, differences associated with social and cultural organization, industrial structure, union organization, the prevalence of part-time work and labor market organization, among other factors. Women are particularly likely to remain excluded from certain service occupations, where the job has retained its craft and skilled status or where men are still interested in maintaining access to service or clerical careers. (United Nations, 1995, pp: 9-10)

Although there is a growth in the number of enterprises owned by women, these enterprises tend to be concentrated in activities with lower rates of return and face difficulties in expansion of business. For example, in China, women represent about one third of the 14 million self-employed persons. The size of their enterprises tends to be small, and their incomes lag behind that of men because of the size and types of their businesses.

In developing countries, women comprise 67 percent of the agricultural labor force. In Sub-Saharan Africa, almost 80 percent of all economically active women are in the agricultural sector. Women produce an estimated 70 percent of the continent's food. Rural women in developing countries tend to be consistently difficult to reach with development resources. According to the International Fund for Agricultural Development (IFAD), in 1990, only 5 percent of the 5.8 billion in multilateral bank loans allocated to agricultural and rural development in developing countries reached rural women (United Nations, 1995). "In some African countries, women who account for more than 60 percent of the agricultural labor force receive less than 10 percent of credit allocated to small farmers and one percent of the total credit allocated to agriculture" (United Nations, 1995: 4). A recent study on loan use in Bangladesh reported that only about 37 percent of women retained full or significant control over loan use in spite of the existence of a number of successful loan programs for women in the country. Because of the persistent discrimination against women, the traditional division of labor, and the lack of training, women are left behind in rural areas, assuming increased responsibilities in subsistence food production or domestic livestock labor while their men are either engaged in growing cash crops or leaving for cities to seek for industrial employment. Rural women benefit the least from industrialization and urbanization and tend to be the worst hit by the effects of rural-to-urban migration. Rural-to-urban migration is dominated by men in Africa, Asia, the Middle-East, and some Latin-American countries.

Gender asymmetries in access to land ownership reinforce male control over the resource. Although a number of developing countries have passed statutes legally affirming the fundamental right of women to own land, in practice, reform measures have excluded women in varying degrees from land ownership. Women typically farm small, dispersed, or remote plots of fragmented land. "Land titles are usually registered in the name of male heads of the household and women do not have secure land tenure. The fact that women do not own land may mean that they cannot get access to agricultural support services, particularly credit and extension services where land ownership is a requirement or extension workers are reluctant to work with small, isolated plots" (United Nations, 1995: 14). New agricultural technologies may result in the masculinization of modern agriculture and feminization of labor in subsistence agriculture on the one hand and increase the time needed to transplant crops, weed, and harvest.

Market segregation has persisted, not only in the types of work done and sectors predominantly occupied by one gender, but also in the differentials in unemployment rates. The gender gap in unemployment is large. For example, in Africa, open unemployment rates for women are often double those of men and have been rising. In Egypt, the female unemployment rate in 1991 was 27.8 percent as compared to only 6.3 percent for males. The 1992 unemployment rate was 21.0 percent for women in Sri Lanka, and the rate was 10.6 percent for men. In Pakistan, the 1990-91 unemployment rate was 13.8 percent for women and 3.9 percent for men in rural areas and 27.8 percent for women and 5.9 percent for men in urban areas (United Nations, 1995). Poverty has a woman's face. Of the 1.3 billion people in poverty in the world, 70 percent are women (UNDP, 1995).

The broad definition of unemployment includes aspects of unemployment such as being without work, having looked actively for work in a recent period, and being available for work at once. This definition excludes part-time workers who want to work full-time and those who need one or two weeks before they can start working. If these people are taken into consideration, the overall gap in unemployment rates between women and men would be widened.

Obstacles restrict opportunities for women to have access equal to men in employment. Lack of sharing of household responsibilities and social services poses serious problems and restricts the options for women since the majority of women have to combine economically productive work with the care of their children or/and of disabled or elderly people. The Nairobi Forward-looking Strategies for the Advancement of Women emphasizes that women's economic independence is a necessary condition for their advancement and envisages a wide range of measures to increase women's access to the economy. The group calls for the elimination of all forms of discrimination in employment, including in wages, and for breaking down gender-based occupational segregation and setting out a series of measures to ensure equal access to all positions of employment and equal opportunities for education and training. However, economic self-reliance does not automatically translate into autonomy and power.

Another major problem in the equal access to resources in most developing countries is the unequal access of girls and women to education, particularly to third-level education. Since 1975, when the first World Conference on Women was held in Mexico City, education has remained a key issue on the international agenda. The Forward-looking Strategies for the Advancement of Women to the Year 2000 adopted at the Third World Conference on Women held in Nairobi in 1985 described education as the basis for the full promotion and improvement of the status of women and a basic tool that should be given to women in order for them to fulfil their roles as full members of the society. International Literacy Year (1990) observed that providing equal access to education for women is a crucial area of concern. Attitudinal, structural, and sometimes legal discrimination against women in obtaining education in male-dominated fields is still one of the major obstacles. Educational systems favor boys over girls in many developing countries where the pursuit of universal literacy still lags behind especially for girls and women (World Bank, 1999). Drop-out rates are much higher among girls than among boys. In Brazil, for example, 63 percent of the children at primary school reach second grade; 47 percent make it to the fourth grade. A recent study found that 80 percent of the girls in Mali have never attended school and 60 percent of the girls who attended school dropped out during primary school. Women comprise two thirds of the illiterate adult people in the world. Ninety million girls in the world have no education at all, over 75 percent in Burkina Faso, Burundi, Mali, Niger, Nepal, Pakistan, and Yemen and over 50 percent in Bangladesh, Morocco, and Senegal.

Pursuit of education is a fundamental human right. The link between education and social and economic status is undeniable. Educational background plays a crucial role in the choice of careers. Education is a determining factor that affects women's access to paid employment, earning capacity, and overall well-being. Literacy is the passport to freedom. It is generally agreed that there is an inter linkage between the growing number of women in poverty and their lack of access to social resources. Poverty has a woman's face. Poverty sometimes result from distribution problems (Sen, 1981).

The second aspect that is related to gender equality is autonomy and the freedom to make decisions. Sen (1991) provided an example of freedom and well-being. Consider two persons. One person starved to death out of choice because of his/her religious beliefs. The other person died of hunger because he/she did not have money to buy food. The two persons achieved the same level of well-being, but the first person's freedom is greater than the second person's. Barriers that work against women's freedom include institutional, structural, cultural, and situational impediments. Women's choices tend to be determined by the gender-ascribed roles that limit their freedom to choose. The 1994 World Survey on the Role of Women in Development recognized three factors that are related to the under-representation of women in management positions: the continuing current effect of discrimination, the lack of measures to increase representation and recognition of women's actual and potential contributions to economic management, and the male culture of management.

An invisible but impassable obstacle is the so-called glass ceiling that proscribes women's professional advancement. The term "glass ceiling" first appeared in the *Wall Street Journal* in 1986 to describe the barriers that stand between women and their rise to top echelons. Employment rules, regulations, and performance evaluation systems tend to be gender based. Conditions of work are largely constructed around the interests of men as employees and employers. Corporate culture is still strongly biased against women. A recent study conducted by the Center for Creative Leadership found that women were not usually considered for difficult or international assignments because managers felt women would not be able to cope with pressure. The proportion of women in top governmental decision making positions is still relatively low. Women comprise 6.2 percent of all ministerial positions worldwide. The proportion is even lower for developing countries.

Women are responsible for about 55 percent of the world's work when unpaid economic activities in the household and domestic services are taken into account (United Nations, 1995). Official statistics, however, often ignore the economic value of women's contributions to domestic services in the household, such as childbearing and child rearing, cooking, cleaning, and family care, when official reports recognize only 37 percent of the world's women as economically active. In India, for example, 29 percent of women were reported as economically active in 1990. But when data were re-analyzed to follow the International Labor Organization (ILO) definition, the figure jumped to over 80 percent.

Women also have to face situational obstacles such as family responsibilities as mothers and wives. On average, women work more than 16 hours per day. Data produced by the Danish International Development Agency in the four villages of Iringa region, Tanzania, indicate that 25 percent of women's working hours totaling 14 hours were devoted to farm work, 28 percent to food preparation, 8 percent to washing and cleaning, 8 percent to collecting water and firewood, 2 percent to child care, 15 percent to other activities, and 14 percent to resting (Lugalla, 1995). The Commission on the Status of Women of the United Nations (1995) reported that the burden of the family and the absence or insufficient sharing of family responsibilities by men and society can affect women's freedom to make choices.

Low levels of literacy and lack of opportunities for training are among the structural barriers. According to the 1993 World Education Report of the United Nations Educational, Scientific, and Cultural Organization (UNESCO), almost a quarter of the world's adult population are illiterate, and two thirds of them are women. The disparities remain pronounced in developing countries, especially in South Asia, Middle-Eastern Arab states, and Sub-Saharan Africa. According to United Nations *World's Women Trends and Statistics 1970-1990*, among women aged 30 years or older, illiteracy rates are 93.4 percent in Nepal, 89.2 percent in Pakistan, 98.2 percent in Burkina Faso, 97.9 percent in Mali, and 90.4 percent in Togo. Disparities in literacy rates between rural women and women in urban areas in many developing countries are also astonishing. In Sub-Saharan Africa, three quarters of rural women aged 15-24 are illiterate compared to less than half in urban areas. In Latin America, the rural illiteracy rate among women aged 15-24 is 25 percent, whereas in urban areas, the rate is 5 percent. In Asia and the Pacific, rural rates are double urban rates (43 percent vs. 22 percent). For women in most developing countries, productive labor is almost the single most important resource, yet they often do not have the necessary skills to increase the productivity in both household and market-based production. Women's access to productive resources such as capital, technology, and land is limited. Although women's right to own land is recognized in many developing countries, in reality their control over the land is rare. Custom-bound laws of inheritance, ownership, and control of property tend to work against women.

The third aspect is the power of women in decision making. Why is it important for women to play an important role in decision making? First, it is a question of human rights. Women constitute half of the world's population, and it is their right to have equality of opportunities and treatment in decision-making processes. Second, it is a matter of social justice. Discrimination based on ascribed status and against one gender should be eradicated. Third, it is an essential requirement for the acceleration and effectiveness of development as women are able to contribute their abilities and creativity. Lack of access, freedom, and authority for women is a form of gender oppression and a matter of human rights.

This study has addressed several of the major concerns of feminists with regard to reproductive rights and gender issues. Socialist feminists focus on the need to change the social structures that channel women into motherhood, child rearing, and low-paid, sex-segregated jobs. For more than a decade, radical feminists have opposed the idea of reproductive rights. Petchesky (1990) argues that the concept of reproductive rights is too narrow, and she prefers the concept of reproductive freedom to reproductive rights. In her opinion, the concept of reproductive rights limits the women's liberation problems to those related to reproduction, as if women were wombs on two legs.

The concept of reproductive freedom provides a broader definition of rights, which includes not only reproductive rights but also freedom from social and economic barriers. Factors such as education, the availability of child care centers, and active men's participation in child rearing broaden the choices women have in reproductive decision making. In order to secure broad-based reproductive choices, it is necessary to gain economic and political power essential to force women's issues into the forefront of public issues. The availability of realistic choices with regard to reproduction is more likely to place the decision to have children in the hands of women than in the hands of men. Radical feminists often support separatist movements, which attempt to establish women's cultures, women's economies, and women's polities.

Provisions both at international and local governmental levels are needed to enhance gender equality and promote women's reproductive rights
Reproductive rights for women are basic human rights and women's rights. International feminist reproductive rights movements cast challenges upon neo-Malthusian, population control, and Christian fundamentalist frameworks. Programs to integrate reproductive decision making and women's autonomy have taken shape in the international agenda. International action to implement the strategies and recommendations made by international conferences and conventions has taken place and has been reflected in policy shifts at international and local governmental levels in varying degrees. The United Nations Population Fund is the first United Nations organization to issue guidelines on women, population, and development. The goal is to mainstream gender concerns into population and development. Emphasis is placed on women's reproductive rights, the Safe Motherhood Initiative, and quality of care, including provision for a wide range of family planning methods. In 1987 the Governing Council endorsed the Strategy to Strengthen the Fund's Capacity to Deal with Issues Concerning WPD (women, population, and development) for a period of four years. In 1991 the Governing Council again endorsed the Strategy, with modifications. The ultimate objective of the Strategy is the total integration of women's concerns into all Population Fund's activities and the

increased participation of women in all projects supported by the Fund. To follow the objectives of the Strategy, the Fund has followed two approaches. The first is to mainstream women; that is, women are fully involved both as beneficiaries and participants in all programs and projects, such as maternal child health/family planning (MCH/FP), information, education, and communication (IEC), and basic data collection. The second approach is to support projects and activities aimed specifically at benefitting women and improving their status. These projects and activities include activities seeking to increase the awareness of policy makers, leaders, media, and the general public concerning the importance of women's issues in population and development. As of mid-1994, there were 124 such projects in all regions, with a total allocation of approximately $34.28 million. The United Nations Population Fund also collaborates with other agencies in the United Nations system on women, environment, and development.

The Committee on the Elimination of All Forms of Discrimination against Women was established in 1982. It is the only human rights treaty body exclusively concerned with discrimination based on sex. The committee has begun the practice of making general recommendations on articles of the Convention as well as other issues raised by it. Declaration on the Elimination of Violence against Women adopted by the General Assembly on the Report of the Third Committee declared that CEDAW would contribute to the elimination of violence against women (Resolution 48/104). It recognizes that violence against women is an obstacle to the achievement of equality, development and peace and that it constitutes a violation of the rights and fundamental freedom.

The Commission on the Status of Women implemented the Nairobi Forward-looking Strategies in its session in 1987. The agenda of the commission focuses on coordination, monitoring, and policy formulation functions. Its substantive work is organized around three priority themes per year for the objectives of equality, development, and peace. The commission makes recommendations on issues with a significant gender content and substantive matters to the preparatory bodies for the World Conference on Human Rights and the International Conference on Population and Development.

The Commission on Human Rights, in its resolutions, has drawn attention to the situation of women as well as practices of discrimination against women, the implementation of the Declaration on the Elimination of All Forms of Intolerance and of Discrimination based on Religion or Belief, human rights education, and harmful practices affecting the health of women and children. In its resolution 1994/53 on human rights and thematic procedures, the commission noted that some human rights violations are specific to or primarily directed toward women and that the identification and reporting of these violations demands specific awareness and sensitivity. The commission called on thematic special rapporteur and working groups to address the characteristics and practice of human rights violations that are specifically directed against women and children.

Another human rights treaty body is the Human Rights Committee. The committee concerns specifically the participation of women in political, economic, social, and cultural life. The committee points out that state parties should take affirmative action to eliminate conditions which cause or help to perpetuate discriminations prohibited by the International Covenant on Civil and Political Rights. Actions may involve granting part of the population certain preferential treatment in specific matters as compared with the rest of the population. The committee has developed some jurisprudence relating to the protection and promotion of the rights of women.

The Committee on Economic, Social, and Cultural Rights pays particular attention to the measures undertaken by state parties to ensure the equal rights of women and men for the enjoyment of all economic, social, and cultural rights.

The Commission on Population and Development monitors, reviews, and assesses the implementation of the Program of Action adopted at the International Conference on Population and Development. The Program of Action strongly endorses the importance of gender issues for all aspects of population and development programs and policies. Recommended actions include establishing mechanisms for women's equal participation and equitable representation at all levels of political processes and public life, promoting women's education, skill development and employment, taking positive steps to eliminate all practices that discriminate against women. The program of action also endorses a greater investment in lessening the burden of women's domestic responsibilities and promoting equal participation of women and men in family and household responsibilities, including parenthood, sexual and reproductive behavior, prevention of sexually transmitted diseases, and shared control and contribution to family welfare.

Following the Nairobi Conference, the International Labor Organization (ILO) adopted the Plan of Action on Equality of Opportunity and Treatment of Men and Women in Employment. Of particular significance in the ILO's efforts to implement the Plan is the execution of a multidisciplinary and interdepartmental project on equality for women in employment, including improving the working conditions, training, labor administration, and labor activities. The ILO's efforts are also directed toward increasing women's participation in the delegations to the International Labor Conferences and other ILO meetings; developing appropriate statistical methodologies for the measurement of job segregation and gender differences in wages; and organizing workshops, seminars, and other meetings to disseminate information and promote equality of opportunities and treatment in employment.

The Food and Agricultural Organization (FAO), the International Fund for Agricultural Development (IFAD), and the Industrial Development Organization of the United Nations (UNIDO) have all initiated training programs to enhance women's roles in agricultural and rural development and implemented technical cooperation projects in industrial planning, environment, and energy.

A very important network of Southern women activists and researchers is the Development Alternatives with Women for a New Era (DAWN). Throughout 1992 and 1993, a series of regional meetings and caucuses at the preparatory committees was called upon by DAWN and other organizations such as the Women's Environment and Development Organization (WEDO), the Women's Global Network for Reproductive Rights (WGNRR), and the International Women's Health Coalition (IWHC). The key products of this process is the Declaration of the Reproductive Health and Justice International Conference and an integrated approach to women's reproductive rights as defined in the International Conference on Population and Development (ICPD) (Correa and Reichmann, 1994):

> ... sexual and reproductive rights include certain human rights that are already officially recognized: basic rights of individuals and couples to decide on the number and spacing of their children, the rights to information and accessible services to that end; the right to respect for security of the person and physical integrity of the human body; and the right to non-discrimination and free from violence. (Chapter VII. The ICPD Draft Program of Action)

Programs that incorporate women's reproductive rights and population control at local and regional levels have exerted some impact on the reorientation of population policies. In Brazil, for example, a national Committee on Reproductive Rights worked closely with the National Council for Women's Rights to formulate guidelines on women's sexual and reproductive rights. The Integrated Women's Health Program in Brazil, together with the Policy on Women's Health and Family Planning, extended family planning services to reproductive health services to women (and men) of all ages. India has developed programs to put family planning in a broader dimension of social change and to focus on a long-term, more moderate approach that centers on a good system of health delivery at the grassroots level, together with improvements in literacy, skill development, income generation, physical and emotional security, and respect for human rights (Bose, 1988). In the Philippines, a major umbrella organization for women's associations, GABRIELA, formed a Commission on Health and Reproductive Rights to set policy guidelines.

Over the past two decades, international organizations and feminist movements have made strides in disseminating information and implementing numerous programs incorporating gender empowerment models. An important finding from this study is that reproductive rights are not an isolated phenomenon but are intrinsically affected by the macro-development of gender equality and that socioeconomic development does not automatically lead to gendered relations on equal grounds. Based on the empirical findings and ongoing international efforts, we propose that emphasis be given to the following: first, population control policies should move beyond the mere control of fertility to the promotion of women's reproductive rights and well-being. Analyses of the impact of population growth on economic development and environmental degradation are important, but the top-down approaches to controlling population growth through coercive family planning programs have provoked oppositions and reproductive health and rights concerns. The view that individual rights must be subordinated to the perceived good of the society through authoritarian measures prior to pursuing individual reproductive rights is not supported by the analysis of the causal model. What is needed are more responsive reproductive policies that are dedicated to improving women's reproductive rights and health at the grassroots level together with improvements in literacy, employment, physical and emotional security, and respect for human values, rather than a quick solution to long-standing problems. As Dixon-Mueller (1993) puts it:

> a population (reproductive policy) cannot be considered apart from an equal rights policy. Redefining the content of a population policy in this way should help to pull together different segments of activities working in northern and southern countries on issues of human rights, women's rights, and reproductive freedom. Most importantly, ridding family planning of its population control rationale and substituting a broader reproductive rights and health focus should appeal to the population, health, and family planning communities, on the one hand, and to feminist health advocates and human rights activists, on the other. The joining together of these communities in a common endeavor becomes all the more compelling in the context of a global political environment in which

> threats to women's rights and reproductive freedom are becoming more powerful. Women's rights groups and the population/family planning establishment cannot afford to be divided in their purposes, nor can feminists allow their anti-family planning rhetoric to be coopted by "right-to-life" organizations committed to the abolition of all artificial methods of birth control and to the perpetuation of women's subordination. (p. 219)

Second, international and local governmental policies should set priority agendas to address issues concerning education, employment, and participation on the part of women. Policies should address gender-based structures and ideologies that curtail women's control over their life chances. An equal-rights strategy that explicitly challenges the structural and ideological forces that have denied women equal opportunities and gains would alter the environment in which women would have control over their life choices and the abilities to mobilize themselves as a social group. Women-centered reproductive policies and programs involve a fundamentally different paradigm and orientation. These policies and programs begin with an understanding of women's lives and adapt the social conditions to their life experiences. A gender-specific and right-oriented human development policy would eventually lead to fertility decline and improvement of women's reproductive rights. Third, there are no cross-national boundaries in women's reproductive rights. Organizations and groups should hold dialogues and discussions about the sources of variations in women's reproductive rights in developing countries. International agencies should strengthen the monitoring and assessment facilities. Fourth, mainstream social research has largely neglected the gender content in shaping women's life chances and their reproductive decision making. Data that are available are fragmented and hardly capture the horizontal and longitudinal dimensions of women's reproductive rights and the forces of gender relations in society and within the family in influencing women's reproductive decision making. Data collection should focus on developing valid measures of human rights, women's rights, and reproductive rights.

As indicated earlier, the International Conference on Population and Development (ICPD), Cairo, marked a remarkable turn around from the previous population ideologies which were oriented toward meeting demographic targets. A new ideology founded on the basis of reproductive freedom and reproductive health for women took shape in Cairo. The immediate consequence of this shift in ideology is a dramatic increase in demand for new types of inputs different from resources required for achieving demographic goals set by population control programs. The fundamental requirement for addressing issues of reproductive health and rights, the ICPD documents suggests, is development. This conceptual link between rights, health and development was strongly advocated by the Cairo agenda. The model of reproductive right we proposed and the results we have presented of the empirical evaluation of the model are relevant and useful for policy makers and researchers in the Post Cairo era. This is because our model of reproductive rights was based on the basic assumption of the Cairo agenda that fertility, reproductive rights and development are linked. The three desired goals for any population control program, the Cairo agenda suggests, should be to improve reproductive health, women's empowerment, and reproductive rights.

The immediate limitation of our model, from a post Cairo perspective is that we have not addressed the issue of health. There is a strong and well-known link between reproductive rights and reproductive health. In this study, the health movement was seen as a source and a catalyst in the emergence of reproductive rights. Yet, reproductive health was not explicitly specified as a correlate of reproductive rights. One of the consequences of this omission is specification error in the model. This is an empirical issue. On the substantive side, and perhaps in our defense, it is argued that high level of reproductive health in a population is likely to be brought about by high levels of reproductive rights. That is, women's ability to make reproductive decision is a precondition for achieving adequate reproductive health. If reproductive rights are recognized as significant antecedents of reproductive health, then our model can be easily extended to incorporate reproductive health as the dependent variable. This certainly is a direction for our work on reproductive rights to grow. The measurement of reproductive rights in the study is based on the rationale established by international conferences and conventions on human rights and women's rights. The definitions and meanings of reproductive rights may vary widely across cultures.

The definitions of reproductive rights from Teheran (1968) to Beijing (1995), on the other hand, emphasize women's individual choices and reproductive health (see Appendix A). The quality of contraceptives and the quality of care women receive in regard to their reproduction are important components of reproductive rights. These definitions may be used as a source for choosing new indicators for developing new scales of reproductive rights.

McDaniel (1996) argues for the need of feminist perspectives for studying social and demographic phenomena. The intersection of globalization with gender necessitates the use of feminist theories to investigate reproductive rights. Folbre (1994) maintains that economic and demographic theories do not pay close attention to women's agency. Development deprives women of their access to valuable social and economic resources (Howard, 1995). In this regard, methodological approaches should pay keen attention to women's life experiences.

As more and more women enjoy reproductive health, there are political outcomes. One of the consequences of the improvement in the level of women's health is an increase in overall women's participation rates in social institutions including those of politics and law. This is likely to bring about an increase in demand for more rights. Thus, the interrelationship between reproductive rights and reproductive health identified in the Cairo agenda remains to be empirically evaluated.

Women's empowerment was seen as a determinant of rights in our model. The focus on women's empowerment is consistent also with the Cairo agenda. Among the three desired goals of a policy to improve quality of life among women, reproductive health, empowerment, and reproductive rights, empowerment is seen as a crucial input necessary to achieve reproductive health and reproductive rights. Thus, empowerment is both a means and an end. In our model, empowerment is specified as a determinant of reproductive rights. To this extend the role empowerment plays in our model is far more limited and constrained than what is envisaged by the Cairo agenda. Future studies may explore the reciprocal relationships among reproductive health, empowerment and reproductive rights.

We have not adequately demonstrated that gender equality is an adequate measure of empowerment. In fact, it might be argued that women's education is also an indicator of women's empowerment. However, women's education has a negative effect on reproductive rights. This casts some doubt on the empowerment approach to achieving reproductive rights and reproductive health. Basu (1997) contends that women's empowerment is too uncritically endorsed in the Cairo agenda. Increases in women's education, and labor force participation have long been recognized as essential ingredients for achieving women's empowerment. Basu (1997) suggests that it is not all too clear that the demand for women's empowerment is universal as assumed. Cultural factors play a crucial role in the way women assess and use power. The lack of cultural variables in our model related to gender equality is certainly a shortcoming from this point of view. Severe data limitations restricted us from incorporating cultural variables in our model. One of the strategies for overcoming this shortcoming is to adopt a comparative study design.

The effect of family planning programs on reproductive rights in our model is restricted to an indirect effect through fertility decline. The direct effect of family planning programs on reproductive rights is well worth exploring. After all, even if traditional family planning programs are oriented toward meeting demographic goals, these programs did contribute toward an increase in contraceptive choices by improving the accessability and availability of birth control methods.

The Cairo agenda identifies development, as an independent source of positive change in reproductive rights. Here again, our results fail to explicitly support this argument. We found that development increases women's education. The effect of education on reproductive rights is negative and significant. Thus, we need to unravel the empirical relationship between development and reproductive rights. One step in this direction is to examine the role of empowerment as an intervening factor between development and rights. In this regard new measures of empowerment have to be developed. In addition, the dissimilar effects of empowerment on reproductive rights across culturally homogeneous areas are to be investigated.

A few methodological limitations have to be recognized and taken into account in the course of either replicating or extending this study. The development of scales for concepts such as reproductive rights and gender equality are essential for adequately evaluating the reproductive rights model. An increase in the number of indicators of these dimensions may increase the reliability and validity of the scales used to measure these dimensions. The selection of appropriate indicators is to be determined by the theoretical and substantive relevance of the additional variables considered.

References

Agassi, J.B. (1989), "Theories of Gender Equality: Lessons from an Israeli Kibbutz", *Gender and Society*, vol.3, no. 2, pp. 160-86.

Alexander, J.(1990), "Mobilizing Against the State and International Aid Agencies: Third World Women Define Reproductive Freedom", in M.G. Fried (ed), *From Abortion to Reproductive Freedom: Transforming a Movement*, South End Press, Boston, pp.49-62.

Anand, S. (1994), "Population, Well-being, and Freedom", in G. Sen, A. Germain and L. C. Chen (eds), *Population Policies Reconsidered: Health, Empowerment, and Rights*, Harvard School of Public Health, Boston, pp. 12-26.

Basu, A. (1997), "The New International Population Movement: A Framework for a Constructive Critique", *Health Transition Review*, vol. 7, pp.7-31.

Becker, G. (1960), "An Economic Analysis of Fertility", in National Bureau of Economic Research (ed), *Demography and Economic Change in Developing Countries*, Princeton University Press, Princeton.

Bell, D. (1994), "The Coming of Post-industrial Society", in D. B. Grusky (ed), *Social Stratification in Sociological Perspective: Class, Race, and Gender*, Westview Press, Boulder, pp. 686-97.

Benda-Beckmann, K.V. (1989), "Comment on Simon and Lynch", *Law and Society Review*, vol. 23, no. 5, pp. 849-54.

Berheide, C. W. and Chow, E. N. (1994), "Perpetuating Gender Inequality: The Role of the Families, Economics, and State", in E. N. Chow and C. W. Berheide (eds.), *Women, the Family, and Policy*, State University of New York Press, Albany, pp.257-75.

Blumberg, R L. (1991), "Introduction: The Triple Overlap of Gender Stratification, Economy, and the Family", in R. L. Blumberg (ed), *Gender, Family, and Economy: The Triple Overlap*, Sage, Newbury Park, pp. 7-32.

Bohrnstedt, G.W. and Knoke, D. (1993), *Statistics for Social Data Analysis*, Peacock Publishers, Inc., Itasca.

Boland, R., Rao, S. and Zeidenstein, G. (1994), "Honoring Human Rights in Population Policies: From Declaration to Action", in G. Sen, A. Germain and L. C. Chen (eds), *Population Policies Reconsidered: Health, Empowerment, and Rights,* Harvard School of Public Health, Boston, pp. 89-105.

Bose, A. (1988), "New Issues in Population Control", in M. Karkal and D. Pandey (eds), *Studies on Women and Population: A Critque,* Himalaya Publishing House, Bombay, p. 80.

Boserup, E. (1970), *Women's Role in Economic Development,* George Allen and Unwin Ltd., London.

Caldwell, J. C. (1982), *Theory of Fertility Decline,* Academic Press, New York.

Carmines, E. G. and Zeller, R. A. (1979), *Reliability and Validity Assessment,* Sage, Beverly Hills.

Chafetz, J. S. (1990), *Gender Equity: An Integrated Theory of Stability and Change,* Sage, Newbury Park.

Charlesworth, H. (1995), "Human Rights as Men's Rights", in J. Peters and A. Wolper (eds), *Women's Rights and Human Rights,* Rouledge, New York, pp. 103-13.

Clark, G. (1994), *Onions Are My Husband: Survival and Accumulation by West African Market Women,* University of Chicago Press, Chicago.

Cleland, J. and Rodriguez, S. (1988), "Marital Fertility Decline in Developing Countries: Theories and the Evidence", in J. Cleland and J. Hobcraft (eds), *Reproductive Change in Developing Countries: Insights from the World Fertility Survey,* Clarendon Press, Oxford, pp. 223-52.

Coale, A. J. (1973), "The Demographic Transition", *International Population Conference,* vol.1, pp. 53-72.

Coliver, S. (ed) (1995), *The Right to Know: Human Rights and Access Reproductive Information,* University of Pennsylvania Press, Philadelphia.

Conterrel, R. (1991), "The Durkheimian Tradition in the Sociology of Law", *Law and Society Review,* vol. 25, no. 4, pp. 923-45.

Cook, R. J. (1992), "International Protection of Women's Reproductive Rights", *New York. University Journal of International Law and Politics,* vol. 24, no. 2, pp. 645-729.

Cook, R. J. (1993), "International Human Rights and Women's Reproductive Health", *Studies in Family Planning,* vol. 24, no. 2, pp. 73-86.

Cook, R. J. (1995), "Human Rights and Reproductive Self-determination", *American Law Review,* vol. 44, no. 4, pp. 975-1016.

Cook, T. D. and Campbell, D. T. (1979), *Quasi-experimentation,* Rand McNally, Skokie.

Copelon, R. (1995), "Remarks", *American University Law Review*, vol. 44, p.1253.

Correa, S. and Petchesky, R. (1994), "Reproductive and Sexual Rights: A Feminist Perspective", in G. Sen, A. Germain and L.C. Chen (eds), *Population Policies Reconsidered: Health, Empowerment, and Rights*, Harvard School of Public Health, Boston, pp.107-23.

Correa, S. and Reichmann, R. (1994), *Population and Reproductive Rights: Feminist Perspectives from the South*, Zed Books Ltd, London and New Jersey.

Defeis, E. (1991), "An International Human Right: Gender Equality", *Journal of Women's History*, vol. 3, no. 1, pp. 90-107.

de Laubier, P. (1985) "Sociology of Human Rights", *Labor and Society*, vol. 10, no. 2, pp. 259-66.

Department for Economic and Social Information and Policy Analysis. (1994, September 5-13), *Population and Development*. Preamble (1.15), Program of Action adopted at the International Conference on Population and Development, Cairo, p.8.

Dixon-Mueller, R. (1990), "Abortion Policy and Women's Health in Developing Countries", *International Journal of Health Services*, vol. 20, no. 2, pp. 297-314.

Dixon-Mueller, R. (1993), *Population Policy and Women's Rights*, Praeger, Westport.

Dixon-Mueller R. and Anker, R. (1988), *Assessing Women's Economic Contributions to Development*, International Labor Office, Geneva.

Dunn, D., Almquist, E.M. and Chafetz, J.S. (1993), "Macrostructural Perspectives on Gender Inequality", in P. England (ed), *Theory on Gender: Feminism on Theory*, Aldine De Grunyter, New York, pp. 69-90,

Durkheim, E. (1895/1958), *The Rules of the Sociological Methods*, (edited by G. A. Catlin), The Free Press, Glencoe.

Durkheim, E. (1897/1957), *Suicide: A Study in Sociology*, The Free Press, Glencoe.

Durkheim, E. (1912/1964), *The Elementary Forms of the Religious Life*, Humanities Press, New York.

Durkheim, E. (1893/1964), *The Division of Labor in Society* (translated by G. Simpson, trans.), Free Press, Glencoe.

Easterlin, R. A. (1975), "An Economic Framework for Fertility Analysis", *Studies in Family Planning*, vol. 6, pp. 54-63.

Easterlin, R. A. (1978), "The Economics and Sociology of Fertility: A

Synthesis", in C. Tilly (ed), *Historical Studies of Changing Fertility*, Princeton University Press, Princeton.

Easterlin, R.A. (1980), *Population and Economic Change in Developing Countries*, University of Chicago Press, Chicago.

Easterlin, R. J. and Crimmins, E. M. (1985), *The Fertility Revolution*, University of Chicago Press, Chicago.

Engels, F. (1884/1942), *The Origin of the Family, Private Property, and the State*, New York, International Publishing.

Fathalla, M. F. (1992), "Reproductive Health: A Global Overview", *Early Human Development*, vol. 29, pp. 35-42.

Fathalla, M. F. (1994), "Fertility Control Technology: A Woman-Centered Approach to Research", in G. Sen, A. Germain and L.C. Chen (eds), *Population Policies Reconsidered: Health, Empowerment, and Rights*, Harvard School of Public Health, Boston.

Ferree, M.M. and Hall, J.E. (1996), "Rethinking Stratification from a Feminist Perspective: Gender, Race, and Class in Mainstream Textbooks", *American Sociological Review*, vol. 61, pp. 926-50.

Folbre, N. (1994), *Who Pays for the Kids? Gender Structures of Constraint*, Routledge, London.

Freedman, L. P. and Maine, D. (1995), "Facing Facts: the Role of Epidemiology in Reproductive Rights Advocacy", *The American University Law Review*, vol. 44, pp. 1085-92.

Freedman, L, P. and Isaacs, S. (1993), "Human Rights and Reproductive Choice", *Studies in Family Planning*, vol. 24, no. 1, pp. 18-30.

Freedman, R. (1961-1962), "The Sociology of Human Fertility: A Trend Report and Annotated Bibliography", *Current Sociology*, vol. 10/11, no. 2, pp. 35-121.

Freedman, R. (1975), *The Sociology of Human Fertility: An Annotated Bibliography*, Irvington, New York.

Garcia-Moreno, C and Claro, A. (1994), "Challenges from the Women's Health Movement: Women's Rights versus Population Control", in G. Sen, A. Germain and L.S. Chen (eds), *Population Policies Reconsidered: Health, Empowerment, and Rights*, Harvard University Press, Boston.

Germain, A., Nowrojee, S. and Pyne, H.H. (1994), "Setting a New Agenda: Sexual and Reproductive Health and Rights", in G. Sen, A. Germain, and L.C. Chen (eds), *Population Policies Reconsidered: Health, Empowerment, and Rights*, Harvard School of Public Health, Boston, pp. 27-46.

Gillespie, D. G. and Seltzer, J. R. (1990), "The Population Assistance Program of the U.S Agency for International Development", in H. M. Wallace and K. Giri (eds), *Health Care of Women and Children in Developing Countries*, Third Party Publishing., Oakland, pp. 526-69.

Greissimer, T.O. (1954), *The Population Bomb*, The Hugh Moore Fund, New York.

Hardon, A.P. (1992), "The Needs of Women Versus the Interests of Family Planning Personnel, Policy-Makers and Researchers: Conflicting Views on Safety and Acceptability of Contraceptives", *Social Science and Medicine*, vol. 35(6), pp. 753-766.

Hartmann, B. (1987), *Reproductive Rights and Wrongs*, Harper and Row, New York.

Heitlinger, A. (1993), *Women's Equality, Demography and Public Policies*, St. Martin's Press, New York.

Hendriks, A. (1995), "Promotion and Protection of Women's Rights to Sexual and Reproductive Health Under International Law: The Economic Covenant and the Women's Convention", *American University Law Review*, vol. 44, pp. 1123, 1138-9.

Hess, B. B., Markson, E. W. and Stein, P. J. (1996), *Sociology*, Allyn and Bacon, Needham Heights.

Homes, H. (1983), "A Feminist Analysis of the Universal Declaration of Human Rights", in C.C. Gould (ed), *Beyond Domination: New Perspectives on Women and Philosophy*, Rowman and Allanheld, Totwa.

Howard, R. E. (1995), "Women's Rights and Right to Development", in J. Peters and A. Wolper (eds), *Women's Rights and Human Rights*. Routledge, New York.

Huber, J. (1973), *Changing Women in a Changing Society*, University of Chicago Press, Chicago.

Humana, C. (1992), *World Human Rights Guide*, Oxford University Press, New York.

Isaacs, S. (1995), "Incentives, Population Policy, and Reproductive Rights: Ethical Issues", *Studies in Family Planning*, vol. 26, no. 6, pp. 363-67.

Isaacs, S. and Cook, R. (1984), "Laws and Policies Affecting Fertility: A Decade of Change", *Population Reports, Series E, 7*, Johns Hopkins University Press, Baltimore.

Jacobson, J. (1991), *Women's Reproductive Health: The Silent Emergency*, Worldwatch Paper 102, Worldwatch Institute, New York.

Jain, A. and Bruce, J. (1993), *Implication of Reproductive Health for Objectives* and *Efficacy of Family Planning Programs,* Working Papers, No. 8, The Population Council, Programs Division, New York.

Joreskog, K.G. and Sorbom, D. (1984), *LISREL Vi: Analysis of Linear Structure Relationships by the Method of Maximum Likelihood: User's Guide,* Scientific Software, Mooreville.

Joreskog, K.G. and Sorbom, D. (1989), *LISREL 7: a Guide to the Program and Applications (2nd ed.),* SPSS Inc, Chicago.

Julemont, G. (1993), "The Status of Women and the Position of Children: Competition or Complementarity?", in N. Federici, K. O. Mason and S. Sogner (eds) *Women's Position and Demographic Change,* Clarendon Press, Oxford, pp. 104-21,

Kelly, W.R. and Cutright, P. (1980), "Modernization and the Demographic Transition: Cross-sectional and Longitudinal Analysis of a Revised Model", *Sociological Focus,* vol.13, no. 4, pp. 315-30.

Kerr, C., Dunlop, J.T., Harbison, F.H. and Myers, C.A. (1994), "Industrialization and Industrial Man", in D. B. Grusky (ed), *Social Stratification in Sociological Perspective: Class, Race and Gender.* Westview Press, Boulder, pp. 659-69.

Keyfitz, N. (1986), "The Family that does not Reproduce Itself", *Population and Development Review,* vol. 12 (Supplement), pp. 139-54.

Kritz, M. M. and Gurak, G. T. (1989), "Women's Status, Education, and Family Formation in Sub-Saharan Africa", *International Family Planning Perspectives,* vol. 15, no. 3, pp.100-05.

Kurtz, P. (1991), "The Secularization of Society", *Free Inquiry,* vol. 11, no. 1, pp. 23-31.

Lane, S.D. (1994), From Population Control to Reproductive Health: An Emerging Policy Agenda, *Social Science and Medicine,* vol. 39(9), pp. 1303-1314.

Lapham, R. J. and Mauldin, P. (1985), "Contraceptive Prevalence: The Influence of Organized Family Planning Programs", *Studies in Family Planning,* vol. 16, no. 3, pp. 117-37.

Lavee, Y. (1988), "Linear Structural Relationships (LISREL) in Family Research", *Journal of Marriage and the Family,* vol. 50, no. 4, pp. 937-48.

Lesthaeghe, R. and Surkyn, J. (1988), "Cultural Dynamics and Economic Theories of Fertility Change", *Population and Development Review,* vol. 14, pp. 1-45.

Leasure, J.W. (1989), "A Hypothesis about the Decline of Fertility: Evidence from the United States", *European Journal of Population*, vol.5, pp. 105-17.

Li, X. (1993), "A Delicate Balance: Concepts of Reproductive Rights and China's Population Policies", *China Rights Forum*, Winter, pp. 4-7.

Loehlin, J.C. (1992), *Latent Variable Models: An Introduction to Factor, Path, and Structural Analysis*, Erlbaum, Hillsdale.

Long, S. J. (1983a), *Confirmatory Factor Analysis*, Sage, Berverly Hills.

Long, S. J. (1983b), *Covariance Structure Models: An Introduction to LISREL*, Sage, Beverly Hills.

Lugalla, J.P. (1995), "The Impact of SAP on Women's and Children's Health in Tanzania", *Review of African Political Economy*, vol. 6, no. 3, pp. 43-47.

Malhotra, A., Vanneman, R. and Kishor, S. (1995), "Fertility, Dimensions of Patriarchy, and Development in India", *Population and Development Review*, vol. 21, no. 2, pp. 281-305.

Mason, K. and Palan, V. (1981), "Female Employment and Fertility in Peninsula Malaysia:the Maternal Role Incompatibility Hypothesis Reconsidered", *Demography*, vol. 18, no. 4, pp. 549-76.

Marx, K. and Engels, F. (1848/1972), *The Communist Manifesto*, Barron's Educational Series, New York.

Mauldin, P. W. and Ross, J. (1992), "Contraceptive Use and Commodity Costs in Developing Countries 1900-2000", *International Family Planning Perspectives*, vol.18, no. 4, pp. 4-9.

Mauldin, P. W. and Segal, S. (1988), "Prevalence of Contraceptive Use: Trends and Issues", *Studies in Family Planning*, vol. 19, no. 6, pp. 335-53.

McDaniel, S. A. (1996), "Toward a Synthesis of Feminist and Demographic Perspectives on Fertility", *The Sociological Quarterly*, vol. 37, no. 1, pp. 83-104.

McDaniel, S. A. (1985), "Abortion Policy Implementation in Canada as a Women's Issue", *Atlantis: A Women's Studies Journal*, vol. 10, pp. 74-91.

Meyer, C.L. and Meyer, C.E. (1997), *The Wandering Uterus: Politics and Reproductive Rights of Women*, New York University Press: New York.

Mills, W. C. (1961), *The Sociological Imagination*, Grove Press, New York.

Moore, W.E. (1965), *The Impact of Industry*, Prentice-Hall, Eaglewood Cliffs.

Notestein, F.W. (1945), "Population - the Long View", in T.W. Schltz (ed), *Food for the World*, University of Chicago Press, Chicago.

Orloff, A. (1993), "Gender and Social Rights of Citizenship: the Comparative

Analysis of Gender Relations and Welfare States", *American Sociological Review*, vol. 58, no. 3, pp. 303-28.

Parsons, T. (1951), *The Social System*, Free Press, New York.

Parsons, T. (1970), *Social Structure and Personality*, Free Press, New York.

Pearson, R. and Sweetman, C. (1994), Abortion, Reproductive rights and Maternal Mortality, *Focus on Gender*, vol. 2(2), pp. 45-50.

Petchesky, R.P. (1990), *Abortion and Women's Choice: the State, Sexuality and Reproductive Freedom*, Northwestern University Press, Boston.

Pine, R. N. (1994), "The Legal Approach: Women's Rights as Human Rights", *Harvard International Review*, Fall, pp. 26-27, 77.

Porter, A. D. (1995), "International Reproductive Rights: the RU 486 Question", *Boston College International and Comparative Law Review*, vol. 18, no. 1, pp. 179-219.

Population Network News (PNN), Fall 1994, no. 9.

Renne, E.P. (1996), "The Pregnancy that doesn't Stay: The Practice and Perception of Abortion by Ekiti Yoruba Women", *Social Science and Medicine*, vol. 42, no. 4, pp. 483-94.

Ritzer, G. (1996), *Sociological Theory*, McGraw-Hill, New York.

Robertson, I. (1981), *Sociology*, Worth, New York.

Ross, L. (1996), "Stop Talking and Finish Women's Treaty", *USA Today*, September 27.

Ross, A.J., Mauldin, W. P. and Miller, V. C. (1993), *Family Planning and Population: A Compendium of International Statistics*, Population Council, New York.

Rosenfield, A. and Maine, D. (1985), "Maternal Mortality - a Neglected Tragedy, Where Is the M in the MCH?", *Lancet, II*, pp. 83-85.

Sassen Koob, S. (1984), "The New Labour Demand in Global Cities", in M. Smith (ed), *Cities in Transformation*, Sage, Beverly Hills.

Sen, A.K. (1981), *Poverty and Famines: An Essay and Entitlement and Deprivation*, Oxford University Press, New York.

Sen, A.K. (1995), *Inequality Reexamined*, Harvard University Press, Boston.

Sen, A.K. (1991, December 5-7). *Welfare Economics and Population Ethics*, Paper presented at the Nobel Jubilee Symposium on Population, Development and Welfare, Lund, Sweden.

Sen, G., Germain, A. and Chen, L. C. (eds.) (1994), *Population Policies Reconsidered: Health, Empowerment, and Rights*, Harvard University Press, Boston.

Sen, G. and Grown, C. (1987), *Development, Crisis, and Alternative Visions:*

Third World Women's Perspectives, Monthly Review Press, New York.

Simon, R. and Lynch, J.P. (1989), "The Sociology of Law: Where We Have Been and Where We Might Be Going", *Law and Society Review*, vol. 23, no. 5, pp. 825-47.

Sjoberg, G., Gill, E., Williams, N., and Kuhn, K. E. (1995), "Ethics, Human Rights and Sociological Inquiry: Genocide, Politicide and Other Issues of Organizational Power", *The American Sociologist*, Spring, pp. 8-19.

Sjoberg, G. and Vaughan, T. R. (1993), "The Ethical Foundations of Sociology and the Necessity for Human Rights Alternatives", in T. R. Vaughan, G. Sjoberg and L. T. Reynold (eds), *A Critique of Contemporary American Sociology*, General Hall, Dix Hills, pp. 114-59.

Sogner, S. (1993), "Historical Features of Women's Position in Society", in N. Federici, K.O. Mason and S. Sogner (eds) *Women's Position and Demographic Change*, Clarendon Press, Oxford, pp.245-84.

Spencer, H. (1884), *The Man Versus the State with Six Essays on Government, Society, and Freedom*, D. Appleton, New York.

Spencer, H. (1897), *Social Statistics*, D. Appleton, New York.

Spencer, H. (1862/1902), *First Principles*, Collier and Son, New York.

SPSS (1988), *SPSS LISREL 7 and Prelis: Uuser's Guide and Reference*, SPSS Inc., Chicago.

Starrs, A. (1987), *Preventing the Tragedy of Maternal Deaths: A Report on the International Safe Motherhood Conference, Nairobi, Kenya, February 1987*, The World Bank, Washington, D.C.

Thompson, W. (1929), "Population", *American Journal of Sociology*, vol. 34, 6, pp. 959-75.

Tonnies, F. (1887/1963), *Community and Society* (edited and translated by C. P. Loomis), Harper and Row, New York.

Turner, B. (1993), "Outline of Theory of Human Rights", *Sociology*, vol. 27, no. 3, pp. 489-512.

United Nations (1973), *Human Rights: A Compilation of International Instruments of the United Nations*, United Nations, New York.

United Nations (1974), *Report of the United Nations World Population Conference, 1974, Bucharest, 19-30 August 1974*, United Nations, New York.

United Nations (1984), *Report of the International Conference on Population, 1984, Mexico City, 6-14 August 1984*, United Nations, New York.

United Nations (1989), *Trends in Population Policy, Population Studies, No. 114*, United Nations, United Nations.

United Nations (1993a), *Demographic Yearbook*. United Nations, New York.
United Nations (1993b), *The Vienna Declaration and Program of Action. Report on the World Conference on Human Rights* (Document No. A/CONF.157/23), United Nations, New York.
United Nations (1994a), *Demographic Yearbook*, United Nations, New York.
United Nations (1994b), *Program of Action of the United Nations International Conference on Population and Development*, United Nations, New York.
United Nations (1994c), *Report of the International Conference on Population and Development, Cairo, 5-13 September 1994*, United Nations, New York.
United Nations (1995). *Report on the Fourth World Conference on Women, Beijing, 4-15 September 1995*, United Nations, New York.
United Nations (1996), *World Population Monitoring, 1996: Selected Aspects of Reproductive Rights and Reproductive Health*, Unpublished.
United Nations Development Program (1992) *Human Development Report*. Oxford University Press, New York.
United Nations Development Program (1995) *Human Development Report 1995*, Oxford University Press, New York.
United Nations Development Program (1997), *Human Development Report 1997*, Oxford University Press, New York.
Veblen, T. (1921), *The Place of Science in Modern Civilization*, B.W. Huebsch, New York.
Veblen, T. (1914/1964), *The Instinct of Workmanship and the State of the Industrial Arts*, Norton, New York.
Walton, S. and Mati, J.G. (1986), "Evaluation of Secondary Infertility in Tanzania", *East African Medical Journal*, vol. 53, no. 6, pp. 310-4.
Ware, H. (1993), "The Effect of Fertility, Family Organizations, Sex Structure of the Labor Market and Technology on the Position of Women", in N. Federici, K.O. Mason and S. Sogner (eds), *Women's Position and Demographic Change*, Clarendron Press, Oxford, pp. 259-84.
Watkins, S. (1993), "If We All Know about Women Was What We Read in Demography, What Would We Know?", *Demography*, vol. 30, no. 4, pp. 551-77.
Weber, M. (1962), *The Theory of Social and Economic Organization* (edited and translated by A.M. Henderson and T. Parsons), Introduction by T. Parsons. Free Press, New York.
Weber, M. (1921/1968), *Economy and Society* (vol. 3), Bedminster Press, Totowa.

Webster, M. A. (1989), *Webster's Ninth New Collegiate Dictionary*, Merriam-Webster Inc, Springfield.
Weeks, J. R. (1994), *Population: An Introduction to Concepts and Issues*. Wadsworth, Belmont.
Weinstein, J. (1976), *Demography Transition and Social Change*, General Learning Press, Princeton.
Weissbrodt, D. (1988), "Human Rights: A Historical Perspective", in P. Davis (ed), *Human Rights*, Routledge, New York.
Whitty, N. (1996), The Mind, the Body, and Reproductive Health Information, *Human Rights Quarterly*, vol. 18, pp. 224-39.
Winikoff, B. and Sullivan, M. (1987), Assessing the Role of Family Planning in Reducing Maternal Mortality, *Study in Family Planning*, vol. 18, pp. 128-43.
Wolf, D. L. (1992), *Factory Daughters: Gender, Household Dynamics, and Rural Industrialization in Java*, University of California Press, Berkeley.
World Bank (1986), *Population Growth and Policies in Sub-Saharan Africa*, Oxford University Press, New York.
World Bank (1993), *World Tables*, The Johns Hopkins University Press, Baltimore.
World Bank (1994a), *Social Indicators of Development*, The Johns Hopkins University Press, Baltimore and London.
World Bank (1994b), *World Development Report*. Oxford University Press, New York.
World Bank (1999), *World Development Report: Knowledge for Development*, Oxford University Press, New York.
World Health Organization (WHO) (1986), *Maternal Mortality Rate: Tabulation of Available Information* (2nd ed.), WHO, Geneva.
World Health Organization (1995), *The World Health Report 1995: Bridging the Gaps*, WHO, Geneva.
World Resources Institute (1992), *World Resources 1992-3*, Oxford University Press, New York.
World Resources Institute (1996), *World Resources 1996-97*, Oxford University Press, New York.
World Resources Institute (1998), *World Resources 1998-99: A Guide to the Global Environment*, Oxford University Press, New York.
Worzala, C.L.(1994), Population Network News (PNN), no. 9, Fall 1994.
Yeager, G. M. (1994), *Confronting Change, Challenging Tradition: Women in Latin American History*, Scholarly Resources, Wilmington.

Young, G., Fort, L. and Danner, M. (1994), "Moving from the Status of Women to Gender Inequality: Conceptualization, Social Indicators and an Empirical Application", *International Sociology*, vol.9, no.1, pp. 55-85.

Zurayk, H., Younis, N., and Khattab, H. (1994), "Rethinking Family Planning Policy in the Light of Reproductive Health Research", *International Social Science Journal*, vol. 46, no. 3, pp. 423-38.

Appendix A

Chronology of the Definitions of Reproductive Rights

1968 Parents have basic human rights to determine freely and responsibly the number and spacing of their children and a right to adequate education and information in this respect. (April 22 to May 13, 1968. Final Act of the International Conference on Human Rights, Teheran.)

1974 All couples and individuals have the basic right to decide freely and responsibly the number and spacing of their children and to have the information, education and means to do so; the responsibility of couples and individuals in the exercise of this right takes into account the needs of their living and future children, and their responsibilities towards the community. (August 19-30, 1974. Report of the United Nations World Population Conference, Bucharest.)

1984 Governments are urged to ensure that all couples and individuals have the basic right to decide freely the number and spacing of their children and to have the information, education and means to do so; couples and individuals in the exercise of this right should take into account the needs of their living and future children and their responsibilities towards the community. (August 6-14, 1984. Report of the International Conference on Population, Mexico City.)

1994 Reproductive rights embrace certain human rights that are already recognized in national laws, international human rights documents and other consensus documents. These rights rest on the recognition of the basic right of all couples and individuals to decide freely and responsibly the number, spacing and timing of their children and to have the information and means to do so, and the right to attain the highest standard of sexual and reproductive health. It also includes their right to make decisions concerning reproduction free of discrimination, coercion and violence, as expressed in human rights documents. In the exercise of this right, they should take into account the needs of their living and future children and their responsibilities towards the community. (September 5-13, 1994. Report of the International Conference on Population and Development, Cairo.)

1995   Reproductive rights embrace certain human rights that are already recognized in national laws, international human rights documents and other consensus documents. These rights rest on the recognition of the basic right of all couples and individuals to decide freely and responsibly the number, spacing and timing of their children and to have the information and means to do so, and the rights to attain the highest standard of sexual and reproductive health. It also includes their right to make decisions concerning reproduction free of discrimination, coercion and violence, as expressed in human rights documents. In the exercise of this right, they should take into account the needs of their living and future children and their responsibilities towards the community. (September 4-15, 1995. Report of the Fourth World Conference on Women, Beijing.)

Source: Population Division, Department for Economic and Social Information and Policy Analysis, United Nation. 1996. *World Population Monitoring, 1996: Selected Aspects of Reproductive Rights and Reproductive Health*. Unpublished.

Appendix B

Program of Action of the United Nations International Conference on Population and Development (UNICPD)

Preamble

1. The 1994 International Conference on Population and Development occurs at a defining moment in the history of international cooperation. With the growing recognition of global population, development and environmental interdependence, the opportunity to adopt suitable macro- and socio-economic policies to promote sustained economic growth in the context of sustainable development in all countries and to mobilize human and financial resources for global problem-solving has never been greater. Never before has the world community had so many resources, so much knowledge and such powerful technologies at its disposal which, if suitably redirected, could foster sustained economic growth and sustainable development. Nonetheless, the effective use of resources, knowledge and technologies is conditioned by political and economic obstacles at the national and international levels. Therefore, although ample resources have been available for some time, their use for socially equitable and environmentally sound development has been seriously limited.

2. The world has undergone far-reaching changes in the past two decades. Significant progress in many fields important for human welfare has been made through national and international efforts. However, the developing countries are still facing serious economic difficulties and an unfavorable international economic environment, and people living in absolute poverty have increased in many countries. Around the world many of the basic resources on which future generations will depend for their survival and well-being are being depleted and environmental degradation is intensifying, driven by unsustainable patterns of production and consumption, unprecedented growth in population, widespread

and persistent poverty, and social and economic inequality. Ecological problems, such as global climate change, largely driven by unsustainable patterns of production and consumption, are adding to the threats to the well-being of future generations. There is emerging global consensus on the need for increased international cooperation in regard to population in the context of sustainable development, for which Agenda 21 provides a framework. Much has been achieved in this respect, but more needs to be done.

3. The world population is currently estimated at 5.6 billion. While the rate of growth is on the decline, absolute increments have been increasing, presently exceeding 86 million persons per year. Annual population increments are likely to remain above 86 million until the year 2015.

4. During the remaining six years of this critical decade, the world's nations by their actions or inactions will choose from among a range of alternative demographic futures. The low, medium and high variants of the United Nations population projections for the coming 20 years range from a low of 7.1 billion people to the medium variant of 7.5 billion and a high of 7.8 billion. The difference of 720 million people in the short span of 20 years exceeds the current population of the African continent. Further into the future, the projections diverge even more significantly. By the year 2050, the United Nations projections range from 7.9 billion to the medium variant of 9.8 billion and a high of 11.9 billion. Implementation of the goals and objectives contained in the present 20-year Program of Action, which address many of the fundamental population, health, education and development challenges facing the entire human community, would result in world population growth during this period and beyond at levels below the United Nations medium projection.

5. The International Conference on Population and Development is not an isolated event. Its Program of Action builds on the considerable international consensus that has developed since the World Population Conference at Bucharest in 1974 and the International Conference on Population at Mexico City in 1984, to consider the broad issues of and interrelationships between population, sustained economic growth and sustainable development, and advances in the education, economic status and empowerment of women. The 1994 Conference was explicitly given a broader mandate on development issues than previous population conferences, reflecting the growing awareness that population, poverty, patterns of production and consumption and the

environment are so closely interconnected that none of them can be considered in isolation.

6. The International Conference on Population and Development follows and builds on other important recent international activities, and its recommendations should be supportive of, consistent with and based on the agreements reached at the following:
   (a) The World Conference to Review and Appraise the Achievements of the United Nations Decade for Women: Equality, Development and Peace, held in Nairobi in 1985;
   (b) The World Summit for Children, held in New York in 1990;
   (c) The United Nations Conference on Environment and Development, held at Rio de Janeiro in 1992;
   (d) The World Conference on Nutrition, held at Rome in 1992;
   (e) The World Conference on Human Rights, held at Vienna in 1993;
   (f) The International Year of the World's Indigenous People, 1993, which would lead to the International Decade of the World's Indigenous People;
   (g) The Global Conference for the Sustainable Development of Small Island Developing States, held in Barbados in 1994;
   (h) The International Year of the Family, 1994.

7. The Conference outcomes are closely related to and will make significant contributions to other major conferences in 1995 and 1996, such as the World Summit for Social Development, the Fourth World Conference on Women, the Second United Nations Conference on Human Settlements (Habitat II), the elaboration of the Agenda for Development, as well as the celebration of the fiftieth anniversary of the United Nations. These events are expected to highlight further the call of the 1994 Conference for greater investments in people, and for a new action agenda for the empowerment of women to ensure their full participation at all levels in the social, economic and political lives of their communities.

8. Over the past 20 years, many parts of the world have undergone remarkable demographic, social, economic, environmental and political change. Many countries have made substantial progress in expanding access to reproductive health care and lowering birth rates, as well as in lowering death rates and raising education and income levels, including the educational and economic status of women. While the advances of the last two decades in areas such as increased use of contraception, decreased maternal mortality, implemented

sustainable development plans and projects and enhanced education programs provide a basis for optimism about successful implementation of this program of action, much remains to be accomplished. The world as a whole has changed in ways that create important new opportunities for addressing population and development issues. Among the most significant are the major shifts in attitude among the world's people and their leaders in regard to reproductive health, family planning and population growth, resulting, inter alia, in the new comprehensive concept of reproductive health, including family planning and sexual health, as defined in the Program of Action. A particularly encouraging trend has been the strengthening of political commitment to population-related policies and family planning programs by many governments. In this regard, sustained economic growth in the context of sustainable development will enhance the ability of countries to meet the pressures of expected population growth; will facilitate the demographic transition in countries where there is an imbalance between demographic rates and social, economic and environmental goals; and will permit the balance and integration of the population dimension into other development-related policies.

9. The population and development objectives and actions of the present Program of Action will collectively address the critical challenges and interrelationships between population and sustained economic growth in the context of sustainable development. In order to do so, adequate mobilization of resources at the national and international level will be required as well as new and additional resources to the developing countries from all available funding mechanisms, including multilateral, bilateral and private sources. Financial resources are also required to strengthen the capacity of national, regional, subregional and international institutions to implement this Program of Action.

10. The two decades ahead are likely to produce a further shift of rural populations to urban areas as well as continued high levels of migration between countries. These migrations are an important part of the economic transformations occurring around the world, and they present serious new challenges. Therefore, these issues must be addressed with more emphasis within population and development policies. By the year 2015, nearly 56 per cent of the global population is expected to live in urban areas, compared to under 45 per cent in 1994. The most rapid rates of urbanization will occur in the developing countries. The urban population of the developing regions was just 26 per cent in 1975, but is projected to rise to 50 per cent by 2015. This change will place

enormous strain on existing social services and infrastructure, much of which will not be able to expand at the same rate as that of urbanization.

11. Intensified efforts are needed in the coming 5, 10 and 20 years, in a range of population and development activities, bearing in mind the crucial contribution that early stabilization of the world population would make towards the achievement of sustainable development. The present Program of Action addresses all those issues, and more, in a comprehensive and integrated framework designed to improve the quality of life of the current world population and its future generations. The recommendations for action are made in a spirit of consensus and international cooperation, recognizing that the formulation and implementation of population-related policies is the responsibility of each country and should take into account the economic, social, and environmental diversity of conditions in each country, with full respect for the various religious and ethical values, cultural backgrounds and philosophical convictions of its people, as well as the shared but differentiated responsibilities of all the world's people for a common future.

12. The present Program of Action recommends to the international community a set of important population and development objectives, including both qualitative and quantitative goals that are mutually supportive and are of critical importance to these objectives. Among these objectives and goals are: sustained economic growth in the context of sustainable development; education, especially for girls; gender equity and equality; infant, child and maternal mortality reduction; and the provision of universal access to reproductive health services, including family planning and sexual health.

13. Many of the quantitative and qualitative goals of the present Program of Action clearly require additional resources, some of which could become available from a reordering of priorities at the individual, national and international levels. However, none of the actions required-nor all of them combined - is expensive in the context of either current global development or military expenditures. A few would require little or no additional financial resources, in that they involve changes in lifestyles, social norms or government policies that can be largely brought about and sustained through greater citizen action and political leadership. But to meet the resource needs of those actions that do require increased expenditures over the next two decades, additional commitments will be required on the part of both developing and developed countries. This will be particularly difficult in the case of some developing

countries and some countries with economies in transition that are experiencing extreme resource constraints.

14. The present Program of Action recognizes that over the next 20 years Governments are not expected to meet the goals and objectives of the International Conference on Population and Development single-handedly. All members of and groups in society have the right, and indeed the responsibility, to play an active part in efforts to reach those goals. The increased level of interest manifested by non-governmental organizations, first in the context of the United Nations Conference on Environment and Development and the World Conference on Human Rights, and now in these deliberations, reflects an important and in many places rapid change in the relationship between Governments and a variety of non-governmental institutions. In nearly all countries new partnerships are emerging between Government, business, non-governmental organizations and community groups, which will have a direct and positive bearing on the implementation of the present Program of Action.

15. While the International Conference on Population and Development does not create any new international human rights, it affirms the application of universally recognized human rights standards to all aspects of population programs. It also represents the last opportunity in the twentieth century for the international community to collectively address the critical challenges and interrelationships between population and development. The Program of Action will require the establishment of common ground, with full respect for the various religious and ethical values and cultural backgrounds. The impact of this Conference will be measured by the strength of the specific commitments made here and the consequent actions to fulfill them, as part of a new global partnership among all the world's countries and peoples, based on a sense of shared but differentiated responsibility for each other and for our planetary home.

Appendix C

Chronology of International Legislation on Human Rights, Women's Rights, and Reproductive Rights

1789   The French Revolution produced The Declaration of the Rights of Man and Citizen.

1869   Geneva International Conference founded the International Committee of the Red Cross (ICRC) for the purpose of reducing the horror of war.

1926   League of Nations Convention.
To suppress the slave trade and slavery.

1945   The United Nations.
With the horrors of Nazi Germany fresh in their minds, the victorious allies came together to create the United Nations, and they were determined to construct a new world order after the massive devastation in Europe and Asia. Among the specific purposes of the UN outlined in its Charters is "to promote ... universal respect for, and observation of, human rights and fundamental freedoms for all without distinction as to race, sex, or religion" (United Nations, 1945).

1948   The Universal Declaration of Human Rights. (International Bill of Human Rights.) It is the first international document on human rights. Adopted and proclaimed by General Assembly Resolution on December 10, 1948, with no dissenting votes, it is recognized as providing the most authoritative definition of human rights obligations.

The International Bill of Human Rights was declared at a time when the international community was eager to construct a new world order after the massive devastation in Europe and Asia and the horrors of Nazi Germany came to an end. It "reaffirmed the faith in fundamental human rights, in the dignity and worth of the human person and in the equal rights of men and women" (United Nations, 1949). Article One maintains that "All human beings are born free and equal in dignity and rights. They are endowed with reason and conscience and should act toward one another in a spirit of brotherhood." Article Three proclaims that "Everyone has the right to life, liberty and security of person." The Preamble reaffirmed "the equal rights of men and women" (p. xvii). Following the adoption of the Universal Declaration, the UN Commission on Human Rights drafted the remainder of the International Bill of Rights: The International Covenant on Economic, Social, and Cultural Rights and The Optional Protocol to the Civil and Political Covenant. These two covenants make the provisions of Universal Declaration into legal binding treaties.

1949 Geneva Conventions.
The first three conventions provided for the treatment of sick and wounded members of the armed forces in the field and at sea, and the treatment of prisoners of war. The fourth Geneva Convention extends protection to civilians in time of war.

1952 The Convention on Political Rights of Women.

1957 The Convention on Nationality of Married Women.

1962 The Convention on the Consent to Marriage, Minimum Age for Marriage and Registration of Marriage.
These three conventions (1952, 1957, and 1962) directly addressed issues related to women.

1968 International Conference on Human Rights (held in Teheran).
The first formal declaration of reproductive rights appeared in this conference. "All parents can decide freely and responsibly on the number and spacing of their children." Reproductive rights are also defined as the rights to "adequate education and information in this respect."

1974 World Population Conference (held in Bucharest). The World Population Plan of Action adopted in Bucharest also included language reaffirming the right to reproductive decision-making: "All couples and individuals have the basic human right to decide freely and responsibly the number and spacing of their children and to have the information, education and means to do so; the responsibility of couples and individuals in the exercise of this right takes into account the needs of their living and future children, and their responsibilities towards the community" (United Nations, 1974).

1975	International Women's Year Conference (held in Mexico). A world plan of action on the equality of women and their contribution to development and peace was adopted. The 1,000-plus delegates at the conference (more than 70 percent of them were women) included the right to reproductive autonomy in their Declaration. In contrast to Teheran and Bucharest, the conference grounded its assertion of the right to reproductive choice on a notion of bodily integrity and control. Article Eleven: It should be one of the principal aims of social education to teach respect for physical integrity and its rightful place in human life. The human body, whether that of woman or man, is inviolable, and respect for it is a fundamental element of human dignity and freedom.
1979	Convention on the Elimination of All Forms of Discrimination against Women. The stated aim of this convention was to achieve equality between men and women in their right and ability to control reproduction, which created a legal basis to address issues related to women's health. It is the most comprehensive international legal instrument to date covering the rights of women. It is the first international treaty attempted specially to address the concerns and rights of women.
1980	World Conference of the United Nations Decade for Women (held in Copenhagen). Focused not only on the themes of the decade but also on three subthemes: employment, health, and education.
1984	World Population Conference (held at Mexico City). The Reagan government did a 180 turn on the population development issues. Rather than urging developing countries to take measures to curb population growth, the representatives of the Reagan administration declared that "population growth is of itself a neutral phenomenon" (United Nations, 1984); that is, the means to quality life was not population control but development, and the route to development was economic growth fueled by free markets and privatization.
1985	The Third World Conference on Women (held in Nairobi). To review and appraise the achievements of the decade for women and to develop strategies for overcoming obstacles still remaining.
1993	World Conference on Human Rights in Vienna strengthened international commitment to the fundamental principle that women's rights are human rights (Pine, 1994, p.26).

1994   International Conference on Population and Development included women's reproductive rights as the empowerment of women in reproductive decision-making over their own bodies.

With the growth of the reproductive health movement, two broad trends were reflected in the Cairo document. First, women's health is important in its own right, because women are not just mothers of children, but they are important, valuable members of society in their own right. Second, women's health cannot be understood as biological processes, but we have to see biology as embedded in, and deeply influenced by, social, economic, and political conditions that affect everyone's everyday life in societies around the world and at all levels, family, community, and state.

1995   The Fourth World Conference on Women (held in Beijing, China) called for the removal of the restraints in women's lives and inequalities in women's participation in economy and policy making.

Sources: Cook, Rebecca J. (1992, 1993, 1995).

Appendix D

A Selected List of International Organizations on Human Rights

International Labor Organization (ILO)

> It was founded in 1919. ILO instruments which are implemented by International Labor Office deal with the protection of industrial workers from exploitation and improvement of working conditions. The ILO also deals with fundamental rights and freedom, such as freedom of association, freedom from forced labor, and equality of opportunity and treatment in employment.

The League of Nations

> It created a mandate system to guarantee freedom of conscience and religion in the former colonial territories of Germany and Turkey.

U.N. Commission of Human Rights

> It is the most important body in the global human rights regime. It has served as the principal forum for negotiating international human rights norms (including the Universal Declaration and the Covenants).

The Human Rights Committee

> It is also a principal body of the global human rights regime. It consists of 18 independent experts established to monitor compliance with the International Covenant on Civil and Political Rights. The principal function of the committee is to review periodic reports, which must be submitted every 2 years.

Appendix E

Convention on the Elimination of All Forms of Discrimination against Women

On 18 December 1979, the Convention on the Elimination of All Forms of Discrimination against Women was adopted by the United Nations General Assembly. It entered into force as an international treaty on 3 September 1981 after the twentieth country had ratified it. By the tenth anniversary of the Convention in 1989, almost one hundred nations have agreed to be bound by its provisions.

The Convention was the culmination of more than thirty years of work by the United Nations Commission on the Status of Women, a body established in 1946 to monitor the situation of women and to promote women's rights. The Commission's work has been instrumental in bringing to light all the areas in which women are denied equality with men. These efforts for the advancement of women have resulted in several declarations and conventions, of which the Convention on the Elimination of All Forms of Discrimination against Women is the central and most comprehensive document.

Among the international human rights treaties, the Convention takes an important place in bringing the female half of humanity into the focus of human rights concerns. The spirit of the Convention is rooted in the goals of the United Nations: to reaffirm faith in fundamental human rights, in the dignity, and worth of the human person, in the equal rights of men and women. The present document spells out the meaning of equality and how it can be achieved. In so doing, the Convention establishes not only an international bill of rights for women, but also an agenda for action by countries to guarantee the enjoyment of those rights.

In its preamble, the Convention explicitly acknowledges that "extensive discrimination against women continues to exist", and emphasizes that such discrimination "violates the principles of equality of rights and respect for human dignity". As defined in article 1, discrimination is understood as "any distinction, exclusion or restriction made on the basis of sex...in the political, economic, social, cultural, civil or any other field". The Convention gives positive affirmation to the principle of equality by requiring States parties to take "all appropriate measures, including legislation, to ensure the full development and advancement of women, for the purpose of guaranteeing them the exercise and enjoyment of human rights and fundamental freedoms on a basis of equality with men"(article 3).

The agenda for equality is specified in fourteen subsequent articles. In its approach, the Convention covers three dimensions of the situation of women. Civil rights and the legal status of women are dealt with in great detail. In addition, and unlike other human rights treaties, the Convention is also concerned with the dimension of human reproduction as well as with the impact of cultural factors on gender relations.

The legal status of women receives the broadest attention. Concern over the basic rights of political participation has not diminished since the adoption of the Convention on the Political Rights of Women in 1952. Its provisions, therefore, are restated in article 7 of the present document, whereby women are guaranteed the rights to vote, to hold public office and to exercise public functions. This includes equal rights for women to represent their countries at the international level (article 8). The Convention on the Nationality of Married Women - adopted in 1957 - is integrated under article 9 providing for the statehood of women, irrespective of their marital status. The Convention, thereby, draws attention to the fact that often women's legal status has been linked to marriage, making them dependent on their husband's nationality rather than individuals in their own right. Articles 10, 11 and 13, respectively, affirm women's rights to non-discrimination in education, employment and economic and social activities. These demands are given special emphasis with regard to the situation of rural women, whose particular struggles and vital economic contributions, as noted in article 14, warrant more attention in policy planning. Article 15 asserts the full equality of women in civil and business matters, demanding that all instruments directed at restricting women's legal capacity "shall be deemed null and void". Finally, in article 16, the Convention returns to the issue of marriage and family relations, asserting the equal rights and obligations of women and men with regard to choice of spouse, parenthood, personal rights and command over property.

Aside from civil rights issues, the Convention also devotes major attention to a most vital concern of women, namely their reproductive rights. The preamble sets the tone by stating that "the role of women in procreation should not be a basis for discrimination". The link between discrimination and women's reproductive role is a matter of recurrent concern in the Convention. For example, it advocates, in article 5, "a proper understanding of maternity as a social function", demanding fully shared responsibility for child-rearing by both sexes. Accordingly, provisions for maternity protection and child-care are proclaimed as essential rights and are incorporated into all areas of the Convention, whether dealing with employment, family law, health core or education. Society's obligation extends to offering social services, especially child-care facilities, that allow individuals to combine family responsibilities with work and participation in public life. Special measures for maternity protection are recommended and "shall not be considered discriminatory" (article 4). "The Convention also affirms women's right to reproductive choice. Notably, it is the only human rights treaty to mention family planning. States parties are obliged to include advice on family planning in the education process (article 10.h) and to develop family codes that guarantee women's rights "to decide freely and responsibly on the number and spacing of their children and to hove access to the information, education and means to enable them to exercise these rights" (article 16.e).

The third general thrust of the Convention aims at enlarging our understanding of the concept of human rights, as it gives formal recognition to the influence of culture and tradition on restricting women's enjoyment of their fundamental rights. These forces take shape in stereotypes, customs and norms which give rise to the multitude of legal, political and economic constraints on the advancement of women. Noting this interrelationship, the preamble of the Convention stresses "that a change in the traditional role of men as well as the role of women in society and in the family is needed to achieve full equality of men and women". States parties are therefore obliged to work towards the modification of social and cultural patterns of individual conduct in order to eliminate "prejudices and customary and all other practices which are based on the idea of the inferiority or the superiority of either of the sexes or on stereotyped roles for men and women" (article 5). And Article 10.c. mandates the revision of textbooks, school programs and teaching methods with a view to eliminating stereotyped concepts in the field of education. Finally, cultural patterns which define the public realm as a man's world and the domestic sphere as women's domain are strongly targeted in all of the Convention's provisions that affirm the equal responsibilities of both sexes in family life and their equal rights with regard to education and employment. Altogether, the Convention provides a comprehensive framework for challenging the various forces that have created and sustained discrimination based upon sex.

The implementation of the Convention is monitored by the Committee on the Elimination of Discrimination against Women (CEDAW). The Committee's mandate and the administration of the treaty are defined in the Articles 17 to 30 of the Convention. The Committee is composed of 23 experts nominated by their Governments and elected by the States parties as individuals "of high moral standing and competence in the field covered by the Convention".

At least every four years, the States parties are expected to submit a national report to the Committee, indicating the measures they have adopted to give effect to the provisions of the Convention. During its annual session, the Committee members discuss these reports with the Government representatives and explore with them areas for further action by the specific country. The Committee also makes general recommendations to the States parties on matters concerning the elimination of discrimination against women.

Article 1. For the purposes of the present Convention, the term "discrimination against women" shall mean any distinction, exclusion or restriction made on the basis of sex which has the effect or purpose of impairing or nullifying the recognition, enjoyment or exercise by women irrespective of their marital status, on a basis of equality of men and women, of human rights and fundamental freedoms in the political, economic, social, cultural, civil or any other field.

Article 2. States Parties condemn discrimination against women in all its forms, agree to pursue by all appropriate means and without delay a policy of eliminating discrimination against women and, to this end, undertake:

(a) to embody the principle of the equality of men and women in their national constitutions or other appropriate legislation if not yet incorporated therein and to ensure, through law and other appropriate means, the practical realization of this principle;

(b) to adopt appropriate legislative and other measures, including sanctions where appropriate, prohibiting all discrimination against women;

(c) to establish legal protection of the rights of women on an equal basis with men and to ensure through competent national tribunals and other public institutions the effective protection of women against any act of discrimination;

(d) to refrain from engaging in any act or practice of discrimination against women and to ensure that public authorities and institutions shall act in conformity with this obligation;

(e) to take all appropriate measures to eliminate discrimination against women by any person, organization or enterprise;

(f) to take all appropriate measures, including legislation, to modify or abolish existing laws, regulations, customs and practices which constitute discrimination against women; and

(g) to repeal all national penal provisions which constitute discrimination against women.

Article 3. States Parties shall take in all fields, in particular in the political, social, economic and cultural fields, all appropriate measures, including legislation, to ensure the full development and advancement of women, for the purpose of guaranteeing them the exercise and enjoyment of human rights and fundamental freedoms on a basis of equality with men.

Article 4.1. Adoption by States Parties of temporary special measures aimed at accelerating de facto equality between men and women shall not be considered discrimination as defined in the present Convention, but shall in no way entail as a consequence the maintenance of unequal or separate standards; these measures shall be discontinued when the objectives of equality of opportunity and treatment have been achieved.

Article 4.2. Adoption by States Parties of special measures, including those measures contained in the present Convention, aimed at protecting maternity shall not be considered discriminatory.

Article 5. States Parties shall take all appropriate measures:

(a) to modify the social and cultural patterns of conduct of men and women, with a view to achieving the elimination of prejudices and customary and all other practices which are based on the idea of the inferiority or the superiority of either of the sexes or on stereotyped roles for men and women; and

(b) to ensure that family education includes a proper understanding of maternity as a social function and the recognition of the common responsibility of men and women in the upbringing and development of their children, it being understood that the interest of the children is the primordial consideration in all cases.

Article 6. States Parties shall take all appropriate measures, including legislation, to suppress all forms of traffic in women and exploitation of prostitution of women.

Article 7. States Parties shall take all appropriate measures to eliminate discrimination against women in the political and public life of the country and, in particular, shall ensure to women, on equal terms with men, the right:
> (a) to vote in all elections and public referenda and to be eligible for election to all publicly elected bodies;
> (b) to participate in the formulation of government policy and the implementation thereof and to hold public office and perform all public functions at all levels of government; and
> (c) to participate in non-governmental organizations and associations concerned with the public and political life of the country.

Article 8. States Parties shall take all appropriate measures to ensure to women, on equal terms with men and without any discrimination, the opportunity to represent their Governments at the international level and to participate in the work of international organizations.

Article 9.1. States Parties shall grant women equal rights with men to acquire, change or retain their nationality. They shall ensure in particular that neither marriage to an alien nor change of nationality by the husband during marriage shall automatically change the nationality of the wife, render her stateless or force upon her the nationality of the husband.

Article 9.2. States Parties shall grant women equal rights with men with respect to the nationality of their children.

Article 10. States Parties shall take all appropriate measures to eliminate discrimination against women in order to ensure to them equal rights with men in the field of education and in particular to ensure, on a basis of equality of men and women:
> (a) the same conditions for career and vocational guidance, for access to studies and for the achievement of diplomas in educational establishments of all categories in rural as well as in urban areas; this equality shall be ensured in preschool, general, technical, professional and higher technical education, as well as in all types of vocational training;
> (b) access to the same curricula, the same examinations, teaching staff with qualifications of the same standard and school premises and equipment of the same quality;
> (c) the elimination of any stereotyped concept of the roles of men and women at all levels and in all forms of education by encouraging

coeducation and other types of education which will help to achieve this aim and, in particular, by the revision of textbooks and school programs and the adaptation of teaching methods;
(d) the same opportunities to benefit from scholarships and other study grants;
(e) the same opportunities for access to programs of continuing education including adult and functional literacy programs, particularly those aimed at reducing, at the earliest possible time, any gap in education existing between men and women;
(f) the reduction of female student drop-out rates and the organization of programs for girls and women who have left school prematurely;
(g) the same opportunities to participate actively in sports and physical education; and
(h) access to specific educational information to help to ensure the health and well-being of families, including information and advice on family planning.

Article 11.1. States Parties shall take all appropriate measures to eliminate discrimination against women in the field of employment in order to ensure, on a basis of equality of men and women, the same rights, in particular:
(a) the right to work as an inalienable right of all human beings;
(b) the right to the same employment opportunities, including the application of the same criteria for selection in matters of employment;
(c) the right to free choice of profession and employment, the right to promotion, job security and all benefits and conditions of service and the right receive vocational training and retraining, including apprenticeships, advanced vocational training and recurrent training;
(d) the right to equal remuneration, including benefits, and to equal treatment in respect of work of equal value, as well as equality of treatment in the evaluation of the quality of work;
(e) the right to social security, particularly in cases of retirement, unemployment, sickness, invalidity and old age and other incapacity to work, as well as the right to paid leave; and
(f) the right to protection of health and to safety in working conditions, including the safeguarding of the function of reproduction.

Article 11.2. In order to prevent discrimination against women on the grounds of marriage or maternity and to ensure their effective right to work, States Parties shall take appropriate measures:

(a) to prohibit, subject to the imposition of sanctions, dismissal on the grounds of pregnancy or of maternity leave and discrimination in dismissals on the basis of marital status;
(b) to introduce maternity leave with pay or with comparable social benefits without loss of former employment, seniority or social allowances;
(c) to encourage the provision of the necessary supporting social services to enable parents to combine family obligations with work responsibilities and participation in public life, in particular through promoting the establishment and development of a network of child-care facilities; and
(d) to provide special protection to women during pregnancy in types of work proved to be harmful to them.

Article 11.3. Protective legislation relating to matters covered in this article shall be reviewed periodically in the light of scientific and technological knowledge and shall be revised, repealed or extended as necessary.

Article 12.1. States Parties shall take all appropriate measures to eliminate discrimination against women in the field of health care in order to ensure, on a basis of equality of men and women, access to health care services, including those related to family planning.

Article 12.2. Notwithstanding the provisions of paragraph 1 of this article, States Parties shall ensure to women appropriate services in connection with pregnancy, confinement and the post-natal period, granting free services where necessary, as well as adequate nutrition during pregnancy and lactation.

Article 13. States Parties shall take all appropriate measures to eliminate discrimination against women in other areas of economic and social life in order to ensure, on a basis of equality of men and women, the same rights, in particular:
(a) the right to family benefits;
(b) the right to bank loans, mortgages and other forms of financial credit; and
(c) the right to participate in recreational activities, sports and all aspects of cultural life.

Article 14.1. States Parties shall take into account the particular problems faced by rural women and the significant roles which rural women play in the economic survival of their families, including their work in the non-monetized sectors of the economy, and shall take all appropriate measures to ensure the application of the provisions of this Convention to women in rural areas.

Article 14.2. States Parties shall take all appropriate measures to eliminate discrimination against women in rural areas in order to ensure, on a basis of equality of men and women, that they participate in and benefit from rural development and, in particular, shall ensure to such women the right:
    (a) to participate in the elaboration and implementation of development planning at all levels;
    (b) to have access to adequate health care facilities, including information, counseling and services in family planning;
    (c) to benefit directly from social security programs;
    (d) to obtain all types of training and education, formal and non-formal, including that relating to functional literacy, as well as, inter alia, the benefit of all community and extension services, in order to increase their technical proficiency;
    (e) to organize self-help groups and co-operatives in order to obtain equal access to economic opportunities through employment or self-employment;
    (f) to participate in all community activities;
    (g) to have access to agricultural credit and loans, marketing facilities, appropriate technology and equal treatment in land and agrarian reform as well as in land resettlement schemes; and
    (h) to enjoy adequate living conditions, particularly in relation to housing, sanitation, electricity and water supply, transport and communications.

Article 15.1. States Parties shall accord to women equality with men before the law.
Article 15.2. States Parties shall accord to women, in civil matters, a legal capacity identical to that of men and the same opportunities to exercise that capacity. In particular, they shall give women equal rights to conclude contracts and to administer property and shall treat them equally in all stages of procedure in courts and tribunals.

Article 15.3. States Parties agree that all contracts and all other private instruments of any kind with a legal effect which is directed at restricting the legal capacity of women shall be deemed null and void.

Article 15.4. States Parties shall accord to men and women the same rights with regard to the law relating to the movement of persons and the freedom to choose their residence and domicile.

Article 16. 1. States Parties shall take all appropriate measures to eliminate discrimination against women in all matters relating to marriage and family relations and in particular shall ensure, on a basis of equality of men and women:
    (a) the same right to enter into marriage;
    (b) the same right freely to choose a spouse and to enter into marriage only with their free and full consent;
    (c) the same rights and responsibilities during marriage and at its dissolution;
    (d) the same rights and responsibilities as parents, irrespective of their marital status, in matters relating to their children; in all cases the interests of the children shall be paramount;
    (e) the same rights to decide freely and responsibly on the number and spacing of their children and to have access to the information, education and means to enable them to exercise these rights;
    (f) the same rights and responsibilities with regard to guardianship, wardship, trusteeship and adoption of children, or similar institutions where these concepts exist in national legislation; in all cases the interests of the children shall be paramount;
    (g) the same personal rights as husband and wife, including the right to choose a family name, a profession and an occupation; and
    (h) the same rights for both spouses in respect of the ownership, acquisition, management, administration, enjoyment and disposition of property, whether free of charge or for a valuable consideration.

Article 16.2. The betrothal and the marriage of a child shall have no legal effect, and all necessary action, including legislation, shall be taken to specify a minimum age for marriage and to make the registration of marriages in an official registry compulsory.

Article 17.1. For the purpose of considering the progress made in the implementation of the present Convention, there shall be established a Committee on the Elimination of Discrimination against Women (hereinafter referred to as the Committee) consisting, at the time of entry into force of the Convention, of eighteen and, after ratification of or accession to the Convention by the thirty-fifth State Party, of twenty-three experts of high moral standing and competence in the field covered by the Convention. The experts shall be elected by States Parties from among their nationals and shall serve in their personal capacity, consideration being given to equitable geographical distribution and to the representation of the different forms of civilization as well as the principal legal systems.

Article 17.2. The members of the Committee shall be elected by secret ballot from a list of persons nominated by States Parties. Each State Party may nominate one person from among its own nationals.

Article 17.3. The initial election shall be held six months after the date of the entry into force of the present Convention. At least three months before the date of each election the Secretary-General of the United Nations shall address a letter to the States Parties inviting them to submit their nominations within two months. The Secretary-General shall prepare a list in alphabetical order of all persons thus nominated, indicating the States Parties which have nominated them, and shall submit it to the States Parties.

Article 17.4. Elections of the members of the Committee shall be held at a meeting of States Parties convened by the Secretary-General at United Nations Headquarters. At that meeting, for which two thirds of the States Parties shall constitute a quorum, the persons elected to the Committee shall be those nominees who obtain the largest number of votes and an absolute majority of the votes of the representatives of States Parties present and voting.

Article 17.5. The members of the Committee shall be elected for a term of four years. However, the terms of nine of the members elected at the first election shall expire at the end of two years; immediately after the first election the names of these nine members shall be chosen by lot by the Chairman of the Committee.

Article 17.6. The election of the five additional members of the Committee shall be held in accordance with the provisions of paragraphs 2, 3 and 4 of this article, following the thirty-fifth ratification or accession. The terms of two of the additional members elected on this occasion shall expire at the end of two years, the names of these two members having been chosen by lot by the Chairman of the Committee.

Article 17.7. For the filling of casual vacancies, the State Party whose expert has ceased to function as a member of the Committee shall appoint another expert from among its nationals, subject to the approval of the Committee.

Article 17.8. The members of the Committee shall, with the approval of the General Assembly, receive emoluments from United Nations resources on such terms and conditions as the Assembly may decide, having regard to the importance of the Committee's responsibilities.

Article 17.9. The Secretary-General of the United Nations shall provide the necessary staff and facilities for the effective performance of the functions of the Committee under the present Convention.

Article 18.1. States Parties undertake to submit to the Secretary-General of the United Nations, for consideration by the Committee, a report on the legislative, judicial, administrative or other measures which they have adopted to give effect to he provisions of the present Convention and on the progress made in this respect:
    (a) within one year after the entry into force for the State concerned; and
    (b) thereafter at least every four years and further whenever the Committee so requests.

Article 18.2. Reports may indicate factors and difficulties affecting the degree of fulfilment of obligations under the present Convention.

Article 19.1. The Committee shall adopt its own rules of procedure.

Article 19.2. The Committee shall elect its officers for a term of two years.

Article 20.1. The Committee shall normally meet for a period of not more than two weeks annually in order to consider the reports submitted in accordance with article 18 of the present Convention.

Article 20.2. The meetings of the Committee shall normally be held at United Nations Headquarters or at any other convenient place as determined by the Committee.

Article 21.1. The Committee shall, through the Economic and Social Council, report annually to the General Assembly of the United Nations on its activities and may make suggestions and general recommendations based on the examination of reports and information received from the States Parties. Such suggestions and general recommendations shall be included in the report of the Committee together with comments, if any, from States Parties.

Article 21.2. The Secretary-General shall transmit the reports of the Committee to the Commission on the Status of Women for its information.

Article 22. The specialized agencies shall be entitled to be represented at the consideration of the implementation of such provisions of the present Convention as fall within the scope of their activities. The Committee may invite the specialized agencies to submit reports on the implementation of the Convention in areas falling within the scope of their activities.

Article 23. Nothing in this Convention shall affect any provisions that are more conducive to the achievement of equality between men and women which may be contained:
 (a) in the legislation of a State Party; or
 (b) in any other international convention, treaty or agreement in force for that State.

Article 24. States Parties undertake to adopt all necessary measures at the national level aimed at achieving the full realization of the rights recognized in the present Convention.

Article 25.1. The present Convention shall be open for signature by all States.

Article 25.2. The Secretary-General of the United Nations is designated as the depositary of the present Convention.

Article 25.3. The present Convention is subject to ratification. Instruments of ratification shall be deposited with the Secretary-General of the United Nations.

Article 25.4. The present Convention shall be open to accession by all States. Accession shall be effected by the deposit of an instrument of accession with the Secretary-General of the United Nations.

Article 26.1. A request for the revision of the present Convention may be made at any time by any State Party by means of a notification in writing addressed to the Secretary-General of the United Nations.

Article 26.2. The General Assembly of the United Nations shall decide upon the steps, if any, to be taken in respect of such a request.

Article 27.1. The present Convention shall enter into force on the thirtieth day after the date of deposit with the Secretary-General of the United Nations of the twentieth instrument of ratification or accession.

Article 27.2. For each State ratifying the present Convention or acceding to it after the deposit of the twentieth instrument of ratification or accession, the Convention shall enter into force on the thirtieth day after the date of the deposit of its own instrument of ratification or accession.

Article 28.1. The Secretary-General of the United Nations shall receive and circulate to all States the text of reservations made by States at the time of ratification or accession.

Article 28.2. A reservation incompatible with the object and purpose of the present Convention shall not be permitted.

Article 28.3. Reservations may be withdrawn at any time by notification to this effect addressed to the Secretary-General of the United Nations, who shall then inform all States thereof. Such notification shall take effect on the date on which it is received.

Article 29.1. Any dispute between two or more States Parties concerning the interpretation or application of the present Convention which is not settled by negotiation shall, at the request of one of them, be submitted to arbitration. If within six months from the date of the request for arbitration the parties are unable to agree on the organization of the arbitration, any one of those parties may refer the dispute to the International Court of Justice by request in conformity with the Statute of the Court.

Article 29.2. Each State Party may at the time of signature or ratification of this Convention or accession thereto declare that it does not consider itself bound by paragraph 1 of this article. The other States Parties shall not be bound by that paragraph with respect to any State Party which has made such a reservation.

Article 29.3. Any State Party which has made a reservation in accordance with paragraph 2 of this article may at any time withdraw that reservation by notification to the Secretary-General of the United Nations.

Article 30. The present Convention, the Arabic, Chinese, English, French, Russian and Spanish texts of which are equally authentic, shall be deposited with the Secretary-General of the United Nations.

IN WITNESS WHEREOF the undersigned, duly authorized, have signed the present Convention.

Appendix F

Hillary Clinton's Remark for the U.N. Fourth World Conference on Women

September 1995, Beijing, China

    Mrs. Mongella, distinguished delegates and guests: I would like to thank the secretary General of the United Nations for inviting me to be part of the United Nations Fourth conference on Women. This is truly a celebration - a celebration of the contributions women make in every aspect of life: in the home, on the job, in their communities, as mothers, wives, sisters, daughters, learners, workers, citizens and leaders. It is also a coming together, much the way women come together every day in every country. We come together in fields and in factories, in village markets and supermarkets, in living rooms and board rooms. Whether it is while playing with our children in the park, or washing clothes in a river, or taking a break at the office water cooler, we come together and talk about our aspirations and concerns. And time and again, our talk turns to our children and our families. However different we may be, there is far more that unites us than divides us. We share a common future. And we are here to find common grounds that we may help bring new dignity and respect to women and girls all over the world - and in so doing, bring new strength and stability to families as well.
    By gathering in Beijing, we are focusing world attention on issues that matter most in the lives of women and their families: access to education, health care, jobs, and credit, the chance to enjoy basic legal and human rights and participate fully in the political life of their countries. There are some who question the reason for this conference. Let them listen to the voices of women in their homes, neighborhoods, and workplaces. There are some who wonder whether the lives of women and girls matter to economic and political progress around the globe ... Let them look at the women who gather here and at Hairou ... the homemakers, nurses, teachers, lawyers, policy makers, and women

who run their own businesses. It is conferences like this that compel governments and peoples everywhere to listen, look and face the world's most pressing problems. Wasn't it after the women's conference in Nairobi ten years ago that the world focused for the first time on the crisis of domestic violence? Earlier today, I participated in a World Health Organization forum, where government officials, NGOs, and individual citizens are working on ways to address the health problems of women and girls. Tomorrow, I will attend a gathering of the United Nations Development Fund for Women. There, the discussion will focus on local - and highly successful - programs that give hardworking women access to credit so they can improve their own lives and the lives of their families. What we are learning around the world is that, if women are healthy and educated, their families will flourish. If women are free from violence, their families will flourish. If women have a chance to work and earn as full and equal partners in society, their families will flourish. And when families flourish, communities and nations will flourish. That is why every woman, every man, every child, every family, and every nation on our planet has a stake in the discussion that takes place here.

Over the past 25 years, I have worked persistently on issues relating to women, children and families. Over the past two-and-a-half years, I have had the opportunities to learn more about the challenges facing women in my own country and around the world. I have met mothers in Jojakarta, Indonesia, who come together regularly in their village to discuss nutrition, family planning, and baby care. I have met working parents in Denmark who talk about the comfort they feel in knowing that their children can be cared for in creative, safe, and nurturing after-school centers. I have met women in South Africa who helped lead the struggle to end apartheid and are now helping build a new democracy. I have met with the leading women of the Western Hemisphere who are working every day to promote literacy and better health care for the children of their countries. I have met women in India and Bangladesh who are taking out small loans to buy milk cows, rickshaws, thread and other materials to create livelihood for themselves and their families. I have met doctors and nurses in Belarus and Ukraine who are trying to keep children alive in the aftermath of Chernobyl. The great challenge of this conference is to give voice to women everywhere whose experiences go unnoticed, whose words go unheard.

Women comprise more than half the world's population. Women are 70 percent of the world's poor, and two-thirds of those who are not taught to read and write. Women are the primary caretakers for most of the world's children and elderly. Yet much of the work we do is not valued - not by economists, not by historians, not by popular culture, not by government leaders. And at this very moment, as we sit here, women around the world are giving birth, raising children, cooking meals, washing clothes, cleaning houses, planting crops, working on assembly lines, running companies, and running countries. Women also are dying from diseases that should have been prevented or treated; they are watching their children succumb to malnutrition caused by poverty and economic deprivation; they are being denied the right to go to school by their own fathers and brothers; they are being forced into prostitution; and they are being barred from the ballot box and the bank lending office. Those of us who have the opportunity to be here have the responsibility to speak for those who could not. As an American, I want to speak up for women in my own country - women who are raising children on the minimum wage, women who can't afford health care or child care, women whose lives are threatened by violence, including violence in their own homes. I want to speak up for mothers who are fighting for good schools, safe neighborhoods, clean air and clean airwaves ... for older women, some of them widows, who have raised their families and now find that their skills and life experiences are not valued in the workplace ... for women who are working all night as nurses, hotel clerks, and fast food chefs so that they can be at home during the day with their kids ... and for women everywhere who simply don't have time to do everything they are called upon to do each day. Speaking to you today, I speak for them, just as each of us speaks for women around the world who are denied the chance to go to school, or see a doctor, or own property, or have a say about the direction of their lives, simply because they are women. The truth is that most women around the world work both inside and outside the home, usually by necessity. We need to understand that there is no formula for how women should lead their lives. That is why we must respect the choices that each woman makes for herself and her family. Every woman deserves the chance to realize her God-given potential. We also must recognize that women will never achieve full dignity until their human rights are respected and protected. Our goals for this conference, to strengthen families and societies by empowering women to take greater control over their own destinies, cannot be fully achieved unless all governments - here and around the world - accept their responsibility to protect and promote internationally recognized human rights. The international community has long acknowledged - and recently affirmed at Vienna - that both women and men are entitled to a range of protections and personal freedoms, from the right of personal security to the right to determine freely the number and spacing of the children they bear. No one should be forced to remain silent for fear of religious or political persecution, arrest, abuse or torture. Tragically, women are most often the ones whose human rights continue to be used as an instrument of armed conflict. Women and children make up a large majority of the world's refugees. And when women are excluded from the political process, they become even more vulnerable to abuse. I believe that, on the eve of a new millennium, it is time to break our silence. It is time for us to say here in Beijing, and the world to hear, that is no longer acceptable to discuss women's rights as separate from human rights. These abuses have continued because for too long, the history of women has been a history of silence. Even today, there are those who are trying to silence our words. The voices of this conference and of the women at Hairou must be heard loud and clear. It is a violation of human rights when babies are denied food, or drowned, or suffocated, or their spines broken, simply because they are born girls. It is a violation of human rights when women and girls are sold into the silvery of prostitution. It is a violation of human rights when women are doused with gasoline, set on fire and burned to death because their marriage dowries are deemed too small. It is a violation of human rights when individual women are raped in their own communities and when thousands of women are subjected to rape as a tactic or prize of war. It is a violation of human rights when a leading cause of death world wide among women ages 14 to 44 is the violation they are subjected to in their own homes. It is a violation of human rights when young girls are brutalized by the painful and degrading practice of genital mutilation. It is a violation of human rights when women are denied the right to plan their own families, and that includes being forced to have to have abortions or being sterilized against their will. If there is one message that echoes forth from this conference, it is that human rights are women's rights ... And women's rights are human rights. Let us not forget that among those rights are the right to speak freely. And the right to be heard. Women must enjoy the right to participate fully in the social and political lives of their countries if we want freedom and democracy to thrive and endure. It is indefensible that many women in on-governmental organizations who wished to participate in this conference have not been able to attend - or have been prohibited from fully taking part.

Let me be clear. Freedom means that right of the people to assemble, organize, and debate openly. It means respecting the views of those who may disagree with the views of those who may disagree with the views of their governments. It means not taking citizens away from their loved ones and jailing them, mistreating them, or denying them their freedom or dignity because of the peaceful expression of their ideas and opinions.

In my country, we recently celebrated the anniversary of women's suffrage. It took 150 years after the signing of our Declaration of Independence for women to win the right to vote. It took 72 years of organized struggle on the part of many courageous women and men. It was one of America's most divisive philosophical wars. But it was a bloodless war. Suffrage was achieved without a shot fired. We have also been reminded in V-J Day observances last weekend, of the good that comes when men and women join together to combat the forces of tyranny and build a better world. But we have not solved older, deeply-rooted problems that continue to diminish the potential of half the world's population.

Now it is time to act on behalf of women everywhere, if we take bold steps to better the lives of children and families too. Families rely on mothers and wives for emotional support and care; families rely on women for labor in the home; and increasingly, families rely on women for income needed to raise healthy children and care for other relatives. As long as discrimination and inequalities remain so commonplace around the world - as long as girls and women are valued less, fed less, fed last, overworked, underpaid, not schooled and subjected to violence in and out of their homes - the potential of the human family to create a peaceful, prosperous world will not be realized. Let this conference be our - and the world's - call to action. And let us heed the call so that we can create a world in which every woman is treated with respect and dignity, every boy and girl is loved and cared for equally, and every family has the hope of a strong and stable future.

Thank you very much. God's blessings on you, your work and all who will benefit from it.

Source: The White House, The First Lady's Press Office.

Index

Abortion right 56, 61,64, 67, 68, 73, 75, 76-79, 82, 83, 85, 100, 108, 110, 112, 114, 115, 120-121
Adaptation 40
Adult literacy 56, 60, 62, 67-69, 72-74, 84, 87
Afghanistan 75, 76, 81
Agassi, J.B. 123
Age of Reason 54
AGIL 40, 41
Agriculture 47, 56, 60, 62, 67-68, 71, 72, 74, 87, 107, 123-125
Alexander, J. 34
Alienation 38, 39
Almquist, E.M. 123
Anand, S. 14
Antigovernment individualism 37
Asia 59, 75-84, 110, 120, 122, 124, 128, 159
Authority 13, 39, 51, 54, 128
Autonomy 45, 48, 51, 62, 117, 118, 123, 125, 126, 129, 161

Bangladesh 9, 30, 75, 81, 124, 126, 182
Basu, A. 136
Becker, G. 49
Beijing 2, 6, 27, 28, 135
Benda-Beckmann, K.V. 7
Berheide, C. W. 122

Bill of Rights 17, 20, 21, 23, 160, 165
Birth Control 1, 2, 5, 13, 43, 46, 49, 134, 137
Birth weight 32
Blumberg, R L. 54
Bohrnstedt, G.W. 65, 66
Boland, R. 23, 25
Bose, A. 133
Boserup, E. 47
Bourgeoisie 38, 39
Bruce, J. 46
Bucharest 6, 12, 28, 151, 154, 160, 161
Bureaucracy/Bureaucratic 39, 41, 69

Cairo 2, 6, 11, 12, 28, 31, 34, 36, 122, 134-137, 152, 162
Caldwell, J. C. 46
Campbell, D. T. 87
Carmines, E. G. 87
Causal effects 93, 94, 106
Chafetz, J. 63, 123
Charlesworth, H. 4, 5
China 9, 13, 27, 30, 32, 71, 75, 81, 124, 162, 181
Chow. E. N. 122
Civil society 18
Clark, G. 122
Claro, A. 34
Class conflict 39

Class consciousness 39
Cleland, J. 49
Clinton, H 181
Cluster analysis 79, 81, 82, 120
Coale, A. J. 47, 49, 57
Collective consciousness 37
Commission on the Status of Women (CSW) 1, 23, 127, 130, 165, 177
Community work 45
Compulsory gynecological examinations 13
Conceptual model 41
Confirmatory factor analysis 39, 68, 88, 91
Consensual unions 45
Construct validity 91
Conterrel, R. 39
Contraception 60, 62, 69, 85, 101, 117, 156
Contraceptive revolution 46
Contraceptive services 13, 14
Contraceptive prevalence 34, 56, 60, 62, 69, 71, 72, 74, 87, 88
Convention on the Consent to Marriage, Minimum Age for Marriage and Registration 24, 25, 160
Convention on the Elimination of All Forms of Discrimination against Women (CEDAW) 26, 28, 117, 122, 161, 165
Convention on Nationality of Married Women 24, 25, 160
Convention on Political Rights of Women 24, 160
Convergent validity 87
Cook, R. J. 12, 16, 28, 43
Cook, T. D. 87
Copelon, R. 36
Copenhagen 25, 28, 161
Corporate consciousness 38
Correa, S. 1, 6, 14, 23, 43

Correlation coefficient 87
Cost-benefit ratio 48
Covariation 66, 70
Crimmins, E. M. 47
Cross-nationally 6, 7, 13, 44, 45, 59
Cultural groups 74
Cultural orientations 41
Cultural standards 40
Cultural system 40
Culture of silence 45
Cumulative probit model 101, 106-111, 114
Cutright, P. 52

Danner, M. 63
Death rates 11, 48, 155
Debates on women's reproductive rights 7, 117
Declaration of Rights of Man and of the Citizen 17
Decomposition 93, 94
Defeis, E. 23
de Laubier, P. 17-19
Democratic society 52
Demographic transition 48, 57, 156
Denmark 18, 30, 182
Dependent dimension 64
Dependent variables 67, 70, 106
Descriptive statistics 65, 66, 71
Desocialization 38
Developed countries 7, 11, 32, 158
Development Alternatives with Women for a New Era (DAWN) 2, 123, 132
Diarrhea 32
Dilettantism 38
Discrimination against women 13, 25, 26, 28, 117, 122, 124, 126, 130, 161, 165, 168-175
Division of labor 37, 39, 47, 50, 63, 123, 124

Divorce 57, 61, 64, 67, 68, 73-79, 85-87, 90, 91, 100, 106, 108-111, 113, 114, 120, 121, 122
Dixon-Mueller, R. 34, 37, 38, 41, 43, 44, 50, 53, 61, 117, 119, 121, 133
Domestic duties 44
Dunlop, J.T. 46, 47
Dunn, D. 123
Durkheim, E. 37, 38, 41, 43
Dynamic density 37, 41

Easterlin, R. A. 46, 47, 49
Eastern Europe 13
Economic infrastructure 47
Economic advantages 45
Economic and social rights 17, 18
Economic, social, and cultural rights 4, 20, 22, 131, 160
Economic growth 53, 62, 153-157, 161
Economic indenture 38
Economic inequality 4, 18, 154
Economic security 51
Ectopic pregnancy 31, 32, 33
Educational attainment 52, 119
Egalitarian relationship 50
Empirical support 65, 85, 91, 95
Enlightenment 17, 19
Endogenous variables 68, 70, 93, 194, 103, 106
Engels, F. 38, 39, 43
Environmental degradation 11, 117, 133, 153
Equality of sexes 57, 61, 64, 67, 68, 73, 74, 76, 100, 113, 114, 120, 121
Error-in-variables 67
Expanded submodel 104-107
Extra-familial involvement 45
Extreme cases 65

Factor analysis 70

Family size 12, 44, 45, 49, 50, 101, 122
Family structure 47
Family planning programs 74, 117, 118, 121, 122, 133, 136, 137, 156
Family planning program effort 71, 74, 82, 86-91, 93, 98, 99, 102, 103, 118
Fathalla, M. F. 29, 46
Female literacy 56, 61, 63, 67, 68, 72, 87, 106, 107, 109
Female infanticide 32
Female subordination 50
Ferree, M.M. 123
Fertility control 2, 13, 36, 44
Fertility decline 44, 45, 46, 47, 48, 57, 92, 122, 134, 137
Fertility regulations 60, 68
Fiduciary system 40
Filial obligation 50
Finance capital 41
Fit statistics 96
Folbre, N. 135
Fort, L. 63
Fourth World Conference on Women 2, 6, 27, 117, 152, 155, 162, 181
Frederick, H. 46, 47
Free choices 39
Freedman, L. P. 11, 28
Freedom of choices 23, 41
Frequency distribution 65, 66, 70

Gabon, 9, 30, 33, 76
Garcia, M. C. 34
Gender discrimination 5, 27
Gender equality 27, 36, 44, 49, 50, 51-54, 56, 63, 67, 68, 70, 82, 85, 86, 89-92, 93, 98, 99, 101, 103-107, 114, 115, 118, 119, 122, 123, 126, 129, 133, 136, 137

Gender inequality 54, 63, 120
Gender relations 52, 53, 123, 166
Gender social definitions 63
Genital mutilation 6, 26, 32, 184
Germain, A. 44
Gill, E. 44
Gillespie, D. G. 12
Goodness of fit 97, 98
Government intervention 14
Greissimer, T.O. 11
Gross domestic product (Gdp) 62
Grown, C. 3
Gurak, G. T. 50

Hall, J.E. 123
Hardon 13
Hartmann, B. 4
Health care 13, 26, 28, 33, 123, 142, 155, 172, 173, 179, 181-183
Health services 12, 14, 34, 36, 132, 157
Heitlinger, A. 45
Hendriks, A. 34
Hess, B. B. 52
Histogram 65, 70
Howard, R. E. 136
Huber, J. 48
Human capital 44, 51, 54
Human Development Index 71, 72, 82, 87, 88, 100, 107, 134
Human rights 1, 6, 8, 11, 17, 19, 21, 26, 30, 34, 36, 40, 43, 44, 59, 61, 63, 64, 112, 117, 118, 128-135, 139, 151, 152, 155, 158, 159, 161, 163, 165-169, 181, 183, 184
Humana, C. 61, 63, 73, 74

Ideal types 37
Immigration 69
Immunization 32
Immutable rights 17
Inalienable rights 18, 27

Incipient decline 48
India 9, 30, 81, 127, 132, 182
Individual well-being 2
Industrialization 27, 48, 52, 53, 124
Infant mortality 22, 32
Infectious diseases 19
Infertility 33
International Conference on Human Rights 6, 28, 44, 151, 160
International Fund for Agricultural Development (IFAD) 124, 132
International Labor Organization (ILO) 19, 23, 24, 29, 127, 131, 163
International debates on reproductive rights 117
International peace 20
International Women's Health Coalition (IWHC) 132
International Women's Year Conference 25, 160
Intervening factor 104, 105, 137
Intervening dimensions 63
Involuntary approach 13, 14
Involuntary perspective 14
Iron cage 39
Isaacs, S. 11, 12, 16, 28, 44

Jacobson, J. 31, 36
Jain, A. 46
Joreskog, K. G. 93, 100
Julemont, G. 51

Kelly, W.R. 52
Kerr, C. 46, 47
Keyfitz, N. 50
Khattab, H. 46
Kishore, S. 119
Knoke, D. 66
Kritz, M. M. 50
KS significant 66
Kuhn, K. E. 44
Kurtosis 66

Labor force 12, 29, 39, 47-49, 53, 56, 60, 62, 67, 68, 70, 72, 87, 107, 123, 124, 136
Lane, S. 13
Lapham, R. J. 46, 60, 62
Latent factor 59, 67, 68, 70, 71, 88
Latent variable 56, 67, 68, 70, 91
Latin America/Caribbean 59, 74-82, 85, 110, 120, 128
Lavee, Y. 97, 100
League of Nations 19, 20, 159, 163
Leasure, J.W. 62
Legal norm 7, 43
Leisure time 47
Leptokurtic 66
Lesthaeghe, R. 49
Life chances 47, 52, 63, 134
LISREL 67, 94, 95, 103, 106
Li, Xiao-rong 13, 14, 44
Logit regression 106
Logit modeling 106
Long, S. J. 67
Lugalla, J.L.P. 127
Lynch, J.P. 7

Maine, D. 36
Male dominance 50
Malhotra, A. 119
Malnutrition 32, 183
Malthus 129
Market costs 46
Market segregation 125
Markson, E. W. 52
Marriage laws 76
Marx, K. 38, 39, 43
Mason, K. 53
Mass media 41
Maternal mortality 32, 34, 156, 157
Maternal death 31
Mati, J.G. 33
Mauldin, W. P. 46, 60-62, 64, 68, 69
McDaniel, S. A. 44, 49, 135
MCH 36, 130

Mean substitution 75
Mean-ends rationality 40
Means of production 38, 39, 50
Measurement model 67, 68, 85, 88, 90, 100
Mechanical solidarity 37
Mesokurtic 66
Mexico City 12, 29, 126, 151, 154, 161
Meyer, C.E. 13
Meyer, C.L. 13
Middle East/North Africa 59, 74-82, 110, 120, 121
Migration 47, 124, 156
Military interventions 19
Miller, V. C. 46, 60, 61, 62, 64, 68
Mills, W. C. 39
Modern economic system 41
Modern society 39, 40
Modernization 46-48, 51, 52, 54, 98, 101, 110, 114, 117, 119
Moral codes 50
Moral obligation 19
Moore, W.E. 47
Multicollinearity 65, 66
Multilateral Bank 124
Multimodality 65
Multiple regression 67, 75, 82, 85
Myers, C.A. 46, 47

Nairobi Forward-looking Strategies 27, 122, 123, 125, 130
Natural rights 17, 18
Natural law 17
Nearest neighborhood approach 82
Need-disposition 41
Nepal 9, 30, 75, 81, 126, 128
Netherlands 69
Niger 9, 33, 81, 126
Nigeria 9, 30, 32, 33, 81
Nongovernmental organizations (NGOs) 12, 179
Normality 65, 66, 71, 97, 100

Normative constraints 37
Notestein, F.W. 48
Nowrojee, S. 44

Observed variables 63, 64, 67, 68, 70, 88, 91, 100,
Observed indicators 66
Organic solidarity 37, 57
Orloff, A. 44
Outlier 66
Overall model fit 95, 98
Overpopulation 11, 14

Paid employment 45, 54, 126
Pakistan 9, 30, 75, 76, 81, 125, 126, 128
Palan, V. 53
Parameter estimates 91, 94, 95, 97, 103, 106, 108
Parsimonious model 105, 106, 110
Parsons, T. 17, 40, 41, 42, 44
Path analysis 110
Path coefficients 114
Patriarchal structures 12
Patriarchal society 50, 53
Pattern maintenance 40
Pearson, R. 122
Pelvic inflammatory diseases 31, 33
Personal security 3, 14, 183
Personality system 40
Petchesky, R. 6, 17, 43, 44
Pine, R. N. 161
Plan of Action 6, 22, 25, 28, 131, 161
Platykurtic 66
Political-legal equality 56, 61, 72, 87, 106
Political freedom 14
Population and development 2, 6, 12, 29, 31, 34, 117, 129-132, 134, 152, 153-158, 162

Population control 1, 2, 8, 11-13, 34, 43, 117, 118, 121, 122, 129, 132-134, 135, 161
Population growth 11, 12, 14, 22, 34, 36, 44, 45, 46, 48-50, 56, 63, 67, 68, 86, 89-93, 98, 99, 101-103, 117, 118, 121, 122, 129, 132-135, 161
Population Network News 35
Power relations 57
Program of Action 12, 26, 31, 34, 36, 131, 132, 153-158
Proposed hypotheses 65, 95
Proximate factors 104
Proximate cause 32
Proximate determinants 44, 103, 118, 119
Pyne, H.H. 44

Q plot 95

Rao, S. 23, 25
Ratio scale 62, 63
Rationality 39, 40, 57
Red Cross 19, 159
Reduced model 92, 93
Reference category 82
Regional variations 32, 71, 74-76, 78, 82, 85, 100, 120, 121
Reichmann, R. 132
Religion 3, 18, 20, 21, 24, 39, 54, 82, 85, 121, 122, 130, 159, 163
Reproductive health 1, 2, 8, 14, 29, 31-36, 117, 118, 122, 132-136, 151, 152, 155, 157, 162
Ritzer, G. 57
Robertson, I. 46
Rodriguez, S. 49
Romania 13, 30
Root mean square residual (RMSR) 97, 98
Rosenfield, A. 36
Ross, A.J. 46, 60, 61, 62, 64, 68, 69

Index 193

Ross, L. 30

Saudi Arabia 9, 71, 76, 81
Scatter Plot 65, 66
Secularization 52, 54, 56, 59, 60, 62, 67, 68, 70, 86, 89-93, 98, 99, 104, 105, 118, 119, 144
Segal, S. 62
Seltzer, J. R. 12
Sen, A.K. 15, 126
Sen, G. 3
Sexually transmitted diseases (STDs) 13, 33, 131
Simon, R. 7
Sjoberg, G. 7, 38, 41, 44
Skewness 66, 73, 74
Slavery 19, 20, 159
Social-structural Determinants 3
Social-structural factors 7, 43
Social-structural variables 85
Socioeconomic development 36, 43, 44, 46-49, 52-54, 60, 62, 67-69, 71, 74, 82, 86, 88-90, 92, 93, 98, 99, 104, 105, 107, 114, 117, 119, 133
Sogner, S. 45
Sorbom, D. 95, 100
Spencer, H. 37, 38
Standard deviation 66, 71, 72
Standardized parameter 91, 94, 103, 106
Starrs, A. 39
Stein, P. J. 52
Sterilization 13, 60
Stewardship 13, 14, 122
Structural equation modeling 59, 67, 71, 98, 102, 110
Structural functionalism 41
Structural model 68, 91, 94
Sub-Saharan Africa 31, 33, 69, 75-80, 82, 120, 124, 128
Submodel 101, 103-107, 119
Sudan 9, 75, 76, 81

Sullivan, M. 34
Surkyn, J. 49
Sustainable development 27, 153-157
Sweetman 122
Synthetic philosophy 37

Tehran 6, 11, 28
Thompson, W. 48
Tonnies, F. 57
Total fertility rate 56, 63, 64, 67, 68, 73, 87, 118
Turner, B. 7, 43

United Nations 4-6, 8, 11-13, 18-23, 25, 26, 28, 29, 31, 36, 60, 61, 62, 69, 70, 100, 117, 122, 123-125, 127-130, 132, 151, 153-155, 158-161, 165, 175-179, 181, 182
U N. Commission on Human Rights 130, 160
United Nations Fund for Population Activities (UNFPA) 12

Vanneman, R. 119
Variability 65
Variance-covariance matrix 95
Vaughan, T. R. 7, 38, 41
Veblen, T. 43
Vienna 2, 5, 26, 28, 155, 161, 181
Violence against women 5, 6, 26, 27, 30, 130
Voluntary approach 13, 14

Walton, S. 33
Ware, H. 45
Watkins, S. 49
Weber, M. 39, 40, 41, 43, 57
Webster, M. A. 64
Weeks, J. R. 49
Weinstein, J. 48
Weissbrodt, D. 3, 19

Whitty, N. 36
Williams, N. 44
Winikoff, B. 34
Women's Global Network for Reproductive Rights (WGNRR) 132
World Health Organization (WHO) 31, 32, 34, 182
World Resources Institute 11, 36, 60, 61, 69, 70

Worzala, C. 35

Years of schooling 56, 63, 68, 69, 72, 73, 87
Young, G. 63
Younis, N. 46

Zeidenstein, G. 23, 25
Zeller, R. A. 87, 82
Zurayk, H. 46